Confessions of a Textbook Writer

If you promise not to get too mad, I'll tell you a secret. I used to write textbooks.

Yes, it's true. I helped write those big books that break your back when you carry them and put you to sleep when you read them. But let me say one thing in my own defense: I never meant for the books to be boring!

I used to spend long days in the library, searching for stories to make my history textbooks fun to read. And I filled up notebooks with stories—funny, amazing, inspiring, surprising, and disgusting stories. But as you've probably noticed, textbooks are filled with charts, tables, lists, names, dates, review questions . . . there isn't any room left for the good stuff. In fact, every time I tried to sneak in a cool story, my bosses used to drag me to this dark room in the basement of our building and take turns dropping filing cabinets on my head.

Okay, that's a lie. But they could have fired me, right? And I've got a wife and baby to think about.

So here's what I did: Over the years, I secretly stashed away all the stories I wasn't allowed to use in textbooks. I kept telling myself, "One of these days I'm going to write my own history books! And I'll pack them with all the true stories and real quotes that textbooks never tell you!"

Well, now those books finally exist. If you can find it in your heart to forgive my previous crimes, I hope you'll give this one a chance. Thanks for hearing me out.

WHICH WAY

TO THE

WILD WEST?

WHICH WAY
TO THE
WILD WEST?

Everything Your Schoolbooks Didn't Tell You About America's Westward Expansion

By Steve Sheinkin
Illustrated by Tim Robinson

SQUARE FISH

Roaring Brook Press
New York

SQUARE
FISH

An Imprint of Macmillan

WHICH WAY TO THE WILD WEST?
Text copyright © 2009 by Steve Sheinkin. Illustrations © 2009 by Tim Robinson.
Concept developed by Summer Street Press, LLC.
All rights reserved. Printed in the United States of America
by R. R. Donnelley & Sons Company, Harrisonburg, Virginia.
For information, address Square Fish, 175 Fifth Avenue, New York, NY 10010.

Square Fish and the Square Fish logo are trademarks of Macmillan and
are used by Roaring Brook Press under license from Macmillan.

Cataloging-in-Publication Data is on file at the Library of Congress.
ISBN 978-1-59643-626-8
LCCN 2010277961

Originally published in the United States by Roaring Brook Press
First Square Fish Edition: June 2012
Square Fish logo designed by Filomena Tuosto
mackids.com

10 9 8

AR: 6.8 / LEXILE: 940L

For Judy and Nick,
heroic leaders in the fight against
boring history books

Contents

How the West Moved West

Have you ever tried to negotiate a treaty for your country? Maybe not. Well, if you ever do, play it cool. You know—don't act too eager to make a deal.

This would have been good advice for Robert Livingston, the American ambassador to France. On the afternoon of April 11, 1803, Livingston was sitting in the office of the French foreign minister. The two men were chatting politely, until the Frenchman cut in with an offer that nearly knocked Livingston out of his chair.

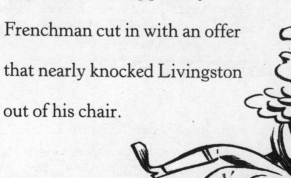

Might as Well Start Here

As Robert Livingston sat in Paris that day in 1803, the United States looked like this:

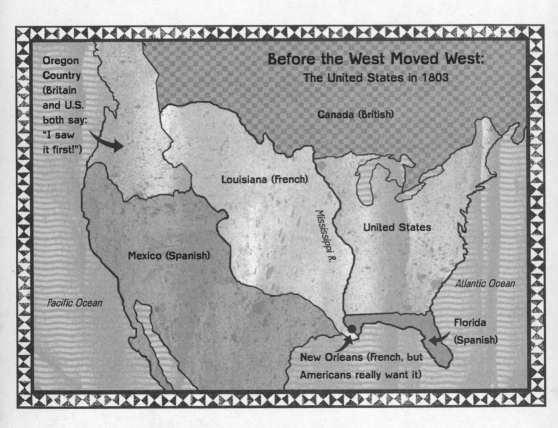

Oregon Country (Britain and U.S. both say: "I saw it first!")

Before the West Moved West:
The United States in 1803

Canada (British)

Louisiana (French)

Mississippi R.

United States

Mexico (Spanish)

Atlantic Ocean

Pacific Ocean

Florida (Spanish)

New Orleans (French, but Americans really want it)

This is a good place to start a book about the American West. Because, as you can see, the land we call the West wasn't actually part of the United States yet. When Americans said "the West" back then, they meant Kentucky and Tennessee.

That was about to change. In fact, Livingston's trip to France set off a series of events that quickly changed the size and shape of the United States—and the location of what we think of as the West. Here's how it happened.

Step 1: Ask for New Orleans

On the map you can see that the city of New Orleans was located in the French territory of Louisiana, near the mouth of the Mississippi River. When American farmers shipped their goods down the Mississippi, their ships had to pass through New Orleans before reaching the sea. This made Americans nervous. What if France suddenly shut this port to American shipping? The French could do it at any moment—they had a much more powerful military than did the young United States.

Terrified of losing their route to the sea, American farmers demanded action from Congress. Terrified of losing their jobs, members of Congress demanded action from President Thomas Jefferson. "Every eye in the United States is now fixed on this affair of Louisiana," Jefferson moaned. "Perhaps nothing since the Revolutionary War has produced more uneasy sensations through the body of the nation."

So Jefferson gave the ambassador Robert Livingston a new assignment: convince the French to sell New Orleans to the United States. That explains what Livingston was doing in the office of Charles de Talleyrand, the foreign minister of France, on April 11, 1803.

Talleyrand listened to Livingston's request. Then he suddenly said: "Would you Americans wish to have the whole of Louisiana?"

This was the point at which Livingston was in danger of collapsing.

By "the whole of Louisiana," Talleyrand meant France's massive empire in North America, stretching from the Mississippi River all the way to the Rocky Mountains. *Hmm,* Livingston thought, *might be nice to add all that land to the United States.* But Jefferson's orders were *buy New Orleans,* not *buy half a continent.*

"No," Livingston finally managed to say. "Our wishes extend only to New Orleans."

But Talleyrand would not drop the subject. "I should like to know what you would give for the whole," he insisted.

Sensing he was being offered the deal of a lifetime, Livingston pulled a number out of the air: twenty million francs (about four million dollars).

Charles de Talleyrand

Talleyrand waved the figure away as if swatting a fly. Much too low, he said. He told Livingston to think it over and get back to him with a serious offer.

Step 2: Send in Monroe

Back in Washington, D.C., Jefferson was getting more and more worried about New Orleans. He had sent Livingston to buy the

4

Robert Livingston

place but hadn't heard any news yet. What was Livingston up to in Paris? What was taking so long?

Jefferson decided to send his trusted friend, James Monroe, to France to help speed up negotiations. When Monroe arrived, Livingston told him that the French had just offered to sell the United States all of Louisiana.

"All France's lands west of the Mississippi!" Livingston said to Monroe. "My, my! Why, no one even knows how much land that is. How many square miles, have we any idea?"

Monroe said he wasn't quite sure.

Anyway, he pointed out, they had no authority to buy all that land. And there was no way to check quickly with Jefferson, since getting letters back and forth across the ocean could take months. By then, the French might have changed their mind and taken back their offer.

Livingston and Monroe talked over what to do next.

Step 3: Buy Louisiana

What the Americans didn't know: Napoleon was desperate for cash. As the emperor of France, Napoleon had the expensive hobby of invading neighboring nations. He needed money for his wars. That's why he wanted to sell Louisiana.

Napoleon told his treasury minister, Francois de Barbé-Marbois, to get the deal done already. He insisted on getting one hundred million francs for Louisiana.

Barbé-Marbois pointed out that this was more cash than the United States government had.

"Make it fifty million then, but nothing less," Napoleon said. "I must get real money for the war with England."

Now it was Barbé-Marbois's turn to play it cool— or, to try to. He waited a couple of days, expecting Livingston and Monroe to come to his office. When the Americans didn't show up, he started to sweat.

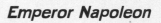

Emperor Napoleon

Livingston and Monroe were still trying to figure out what to do. They invited some friends for dinner and were talking things over when they noticed someone watching them from the garden behind the house.

"Doesn't that look like Barbé-Marbois out there?" asked one of the dinner guests.

"It is! It is!" cried Livingston.

Yes, the treasury minister of France was peeking through their dining room window. So much for playing it cool.

Livingston went to the window and invited Barbé-Marbois to come around to the door. Then the two men had a short, awkward conversation.

Livingston and Monroe realized the French were eager to make a deal. And they took a chance, guessing Jefferson would want Louisiana (he did). Over the next couple of weeks, the American and French negotiators hammered out the details of what became the Louisiana Purchase. The United States paid fifteen million dollars (75 million francs) for the Louisiana Territory—less than four cents an acre.

The purchase instantly doubled the size of the United States, which now looked like this:

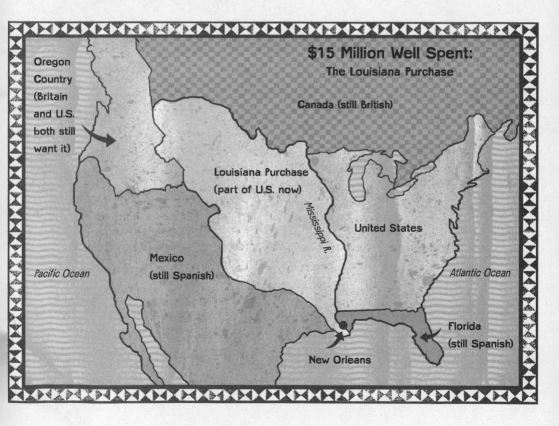

$15 Million Well Spent: The Louisiana Purchase

Oregon Country (Britain and U.S. both still want it)

Canada (still British)

Louisiana Purchase (part of U.S. now)

Mississippi R.

United States

Mexico (still Spanish)

Pacific Ocean

Atlantic Ocean

New Orleans

Florida (still Spanish)

Step 4: Hire Lewis and Clark

O f course, it's easy to draw maps these days. But back in 1803 the Americans didn't really know what they had just bought, or who lived there. Thomas Jefferson gave the job of finding out to two explorers: Meriwether Lewis and William Clark.

William Clark

Meriwether Lewis

York

Lewis and Clark's mission was to explore the land, study new plants and animals, find rivers leading from the Mississippi River to the Pacific Ocean (there aren't any), and establish friendly relations with Native American tribes. The two explorers put together a thirty-three-man team they called the Corps of Discovery, made up mostly of young soldiers. The crew included one African American, a young man named York. (Clark called him "my manservant." Actually, York was Clark's slave.)

The Corps of Discovery set out from St. Louis, Missouri, in May 1804.

Step 5: Meet Your Neighbors

A few months later, three Lakota Indian boys were swimming in the Missouri River in what is now South Dakota. They noticed a group of about thirty men setting up tents on the other side of the river. The boys had seen a few white men before (though never a black man). But they had never seen a large group like this. They swam across the river to investigate.

Though they couldn't understand each other's words, the Lakota boys and the travelers were able to communicate pretty well using sign language. The leaders of the white men seemed to be saying that they wanted to meet with the Indian chiefs. The boys told them to come to their nearby village, and pointed out the way.

Two days later the travelers paddled up to the village. The chiefs welcomed them, and the groups traded food as a symbol of goodwill. Then the Lakota people gathered around to listen to one of the white leaders, who began a speech with the words:

"Blah, blah, blah, blah, blah, blah, blah,

blah, blah, blah, blah, blah, blah, blah,

blah, blah, blah blah . . ."

At least, that's what it must have sounded like to the Lakota. To those who spoke English, it was clear that Lewis was explaining that all of this land now belonged to the United States. From now on, Lewis said, Native Americans of the region must obey the commands of the "Great Chief"— President Jefferson, that is.

Meriwether Lewis

"The Great Chief of the seventeen great nations of America has become your only father," Lewis said. "He is the only friend to whom you can now look for protection, or from whom you can ask favors, or receive good councils, and he will take care that you shall have no just cause to regret this change."

No cause to regret the change? Well, we'll see about that.

Meanwhile, Lewis realized that the Lakota had no clue what he was saying. One of Lewis's men was trying to translate the speech using sign language. It wasn't working. "We feel much at a loss for the want of an interpreter," Clark noted.

So Lewis stopped talking. Instead, he had his men put on their fancy army uniforms and parade back and forth, firing their guns. Then Lewis and Clark gave out gifts to the chiefs—each one got a "peace medal" with an image of President Jefferson on one side and an Indian and a white man shaking hands on the other.

The reaction of the Lakota chiefs was basically *That's it? You're asking to pass through our territory, and all you offer in exchange is a stupid medal?* They wanted useful tools, and guns and ammunition.

Both sides were annoyed. Both sides were frustrated by their inability to communicate. When three Lakota warriors grabbed one of Lewis and Clark's boats, the situation nearly exploded. The Indians and Americans shouted threats at each other. "I felt myself warm and spoke in very positive terms," Clark remembered.

Clark pulled out his sword and ordered his men to aim their guns. The Lakota warriors raised their own weapons. "Most of the warriors appeared to have their bows strung and took out their arrows from the quiver," said Clark.

For several tense seconds the two groups stood fifty feet apart, weapons aimed at each other. Anything could have happened— though if shooting started, the badly outnumbered Corps of Discovery would almost certainly have been wiped out. Finally, a Lakota chief named Black Buffalo stepped between the men and convinced his warriors to lower their bows.

Then the Corps of Discovery continued their journey west.

Step 6: Ask Directions

Lewis and Clark had a much better time at the Mandan and Hidatsa villages they reached the following month. They were given food and information about the route ahead. Most important, this is where they met a sixteen-year-old Shoshone woman named Sacagawea.

About four years before, Hidatsa warriors had raided a Shoshone village and kidnapped Sacagawea. They then sold her to a Canadian fur trader named Toussaint Charbonneau. He considered her his wife (though technically he already had one).

Now Charbonneau came to Lewis and made an offer: Hire me and Sacagawea as interpreters. Lewis didn't really want Charbonneau (he called the fur trapper "a man of no particular merit"), but he did think Sacagawea's knowledge of the Shoshone language would be helpful. Lewis hoped to meet up with the Shoshone in the Rocky Mountains, and he would need their knowledge of the local geography. So he agreed to hire the husband-and-wife team (all the money went to the husband).

On a freezing morning in February 1805, Sacagawea gave birth to a baby boy, Jean Baptiste. Less than two months later, she strapped the baby on her back and headed west with the Corps of Discovery.

As Lewis had feared, Charbonneau was not too helpful. He kept accidentally tipping over the boats, dumping precious supplies into the river. Sacagawea proved to be much more

Sacagawea

12

useful, finding edible roots and berries where no one else would have known to look.

By the time the crew climbed into the Rocky Mountains in August, the men were hungry and exhausted. And lost. Luckily for the Corps, Sacagawea had grown up around there. "The Indian woman recognized the point of a high plain to our right, which she informed us was not very distant from the summer retreat of her nation," wrote Lewis.

Sure enough, Lewis soon spotted a Shoshone man on a horse, about two hundred yards away. "I now called to him in as loud a voice as I could command," said Lewis, "repeating the word *tab-ba-bone*, which in their language signifies 'white man.'"

The Shoshone rider took one look at this group of armed men coming toward him shouting "White man!" He turned his horse and raced away.

The Americans spent the next few days desperately searching for the Shoshone camp. Lewis kept spotting single Shoshone at a distance and then calling out, *"Tab-ba-bone! Tab-ba-bone!"* And they kept riding away.

Finally the Corps found the camp. Standing there waiting for them were sixty Shoshone warriors. Lewis did a smart thing—he set his rifle on the ground.

The Shoshone then strode toward Lewis, saying, *"Ah-hi-e, ah-hi-e."* Lewis was quite confused, until the chief put his arm around Lewis's shoulder and touched his cheek to Lewis's cheek. That seemed like a good sign. (Lewis learned later that *"Ah-hi-e"* means "I am much pleased.")

Sacagawea began to interpret between Lewis and the chief. But she kept stopping to stare at the chief's familiar face. She suddenly realized that this was Cameahwait, her long-lost big brother! "She jumped up and ran and embraced him," Lewis wrote. Sacagawea had not shown the tiniest bit of emotion in the months Lewis had known her. Now, as she interpreted between her brother and Lewis, she kept bursting out in tears of joy.

Step 7: Bring Back the News

Thanks largely to Sacagawea, the Shoshone gave Lewis and Clark advice about how to cross the mountains, and horses to carry their goods. The Corps continued west, making it all the way to the Pacific coast by November 1805. Here Clark wrote his famous line:

"Ocian in View! O! the joy."

William Clark

That was Clark: good explorer, bad speller.

Lewis and Clark headed home the following year. They made it back without any major disasters, unless you count the time Lewis and the nearsighted Corps member Pierre Cruzatte went hunting for elk. Lewis spotted an animal and was aiming his gun when he felt a sudden and terrible pain in his butt. He turned around and saw blood running down his thigh.

"You have shot me," he said to Cruzatte.

Cruzatte denied it, which was silly since the bullet from his gun was clearly lodged in Lewis's leather pants.

So for a few weeks Lewis had to ride in the canoe lying on his stomach. Still, the Corps made it safely back to St. Louis in September 1806. In two and a half years, Lewis and Clark had zigzagged more than eight thousand miles across the West, met with about fifty Indian groups, and found hundreds of species of plants and animals. Reports of their adventures got Americans excited about exploring the West.

Step 8: Become a Mountain Man

One of the things Lewis and Clark reported was that the rivers and streams of the West were filled with beaver. This caught people's attention, because hats made of beaver fur were currently in fashion in European cities (rich folks simply had to have their beaver hats). There was big money in the beaver pelt business. The only hard part: someone had to go get the pelts.

James Beckwourth decided to give it a try. After being freed from slavery as a boy, Beckwourth had moved with his family to St. Louis. When he was twenty-four he heard that companies were looking for daring young men to head west into the unmapped mountains to trap beaver. Beckwourth rushed to sign up.

"Being possessed with a strong desire to see the celebrated Rocky Mountains, and the great western wilderness so much talked about, I engaged in General Ashley's Rocky Mountain Fur Company."

James Beckwourth

Beckwourth was one of a few hundred adventurers who became known as "mountain men." Exploring the mountains and trapping beaver in icy streams, mountain men were often freezing, starving, and lonely. And they were always on the lookout for mountain lions and grizzly bears. Mountain man Jedediah Smith was searching for a route through the Rockies when he was attacked by a grizzly. The bear smacked Smith around like a doll, smashing several of his ribs. Then it took Smith's head in its teeth and shook him back and forth.

Fellow mountain man James Clyman found Smith lying in the bloody dirt. Smith somehow managed to say, "If you have a needle and thread, get it out and sew up my wounds around my head."

Clyman crouched down to have a look. The scalp had been ripped from Smith's skull. One ear was hanging on by a twisted strip of skin.

"I told him I could do nothing for his ear," Clyman said.

"Oh, you must try to stitch it up some way or other," pleaded Smith.

Clyman took out the tools he used to mend his socks and went to work. "I put in my needle and stitched it through and through and over and over," he said, "nice as I could."

Incredibly, Smith's ear stayed on. And he was back on his horse in less than two weeks.

Step 9: Learn from the Locals

Fights with Native Americans were another danger, since some tribes did not welcome the sight of outsiders trapping animals in their territory. But more often, mountain men traded with Native Americans, learning from them how to hunt, travel, and survive in the snowy mountains. Mountain men began dressing like Indians, and they considered it a great compliment to be mistaken for one of them.

James Beckwourth did more than dress like an Indian—he moved in with them. Invited to join a group of Crow Indians, Beckwourth learned the Crow language, got married, and even fought in the Crow's battles against rival tribes.

When Beckwourth's mountain men friends didn't see him for a

few years, they figured he must have died somewhere in the wilderness. This led to a strange scene at Fort Clark, a trading post in what is now North Dakota.

Beckwourth and some Crow friends showed up with a stack of beaver pelts to trade. Of course, they were dressed as Crows and speaking the Crow language. One of the Crow men stepped up to the counter and asked the American clerks for *"be-has-i-pe-hish-a."*

The puzzled clerks just stood there.

"Be-has-i-pe-hish-a," said the Crow.

More confused silence.

Then Beckwourth stepped up and said, "Gentlemen, that Indian wants scarlet cloth."

"If a bombshell had exploded in the fort they could not have been more astonished," Beckwourth remembered. This dialogue followed:

Clerk: *Ah, you speak English! Where did you learn it?*

Beckwourth: *With the white man.*

Clerk: *How long were you with the whites?*

Beckwourth: *More than twenty years.*

Clerk: *Where did you live with them?*

Beckwourth: *In St. Louis.*

Clerk: *If you have lived twenty years in St. Louis, I'll swear you are no Crow.*

Beckwourth: *No, I am not.*

Clerk: *Then what may be your name?*

Beckwourth: *My name in English is James Beckwourth.*

Clerk: *Good heavens! Why, I have heard your name mentioned a thousand times. You were supposed to be dead.*

Beckwourth: *I am not dead, as you see.*

James Beckwourth spent another six years with the Crows, becoming a high-ranking chief. And all the while, stories about Beckwourth and other mountain men continued to excite Americans about new opportunities in the West.

Step 10: Stumble to Santa Fe

This interest in the West gave a nineteen-year-old named David Meriwether what seemed like a good idea. He would set up a trading route connecting American towns in Missouri with settlements in northern Mexico, hundreds of miles to the southwest.

"I had learned from the Indians that there was a good country from Missouri to the Mexican settlements for a road," Meriwether said. The key would be to find a route that wagons could use to transport goods back and forth. In June 1820, Meriwether set out to find the route.

Traveling with him was an African American teenager named Alfred. (Was Alfred his friend? His slave? Both? Meriwether doesn't say.) The problem was, Mexico was Spanish territory, and Spanish leaders didn't allow Americans on their land. Soon after crossing into Mexico, Meriwether and Alfred were arrested by Spanish soldiers.

The soldiers forced the Americans to march through the scorching desert toward the town of Santa Fe. Meriwether's feet were soon sliced open by rocks and cactus needles. "This was the most miserable day of my life," he remembered, "for I felt as though I would as soon die as live."

Unable to bear the pain of another step, Meriwether dropped to the sand and refused to move. A Spanish soldier raised his sword over Meriwether's head.

"Davy, get up and come along or they will kill you," Alfred urged.

"Let them kill me; I will not walk another step farther."

David Meriwether   *Alfred*

Alfred somehow talked the soldiers into letting Meriwether ride a mule. When they finally arrived in Santa Fe, the Americans were thrown into separate flea-filled jail cells. Meriwether was starving by now, so when a guard finally brought in some food he was thrilled— until he tasted it. "About night my jailor came with a small earthen bowl with boiled frijoles, or red beans," he said "I found it so strongly seasoned with pepper that I could not eat it."

Boy, when things go wrong. . . . Anyway, after swearing to go back to American territory and stay there, Meriwether and Alfred were let out of jail.

"I never expected to see you again," Alfred said when they met in the street outside the prison. They quickly headed back to Missouri.

Just a year later, in 1821, Mexicans kicked out the Spanish rulers and declared themselves independent. This changed everything, because Mexican leaders welcomed American travelers and traders. And the route that Alfred and Meriwether had traveled soon became a busy trading route known as the Santa Fe Trail.

Even without angry soldiers to deal with, this was a dangerous eight-hundred-mile trip. One of the first groups to travel the trail found this out when they decided to take a shortcut through the Cimarron Desert. They soon ran out of water and were close to dying of thirst when they saw a buffalo walking toward them. They shot the animal, cut it open—and shouted with joy to find its stomach filled with water. The men gulped down the warm liquid and got back on the trail to Santa Fe.

What's that you say? You like the idea of moving west, but you don't feel like wrestling grizzly bears or drinking buffalo puke? Then you might consider settling on a plot of fertile land in the northern region of Mexico called Tejas.

Step 11: Move to Texas

When Mexico won its independence from Spain in 1821, the new nation looked like this:

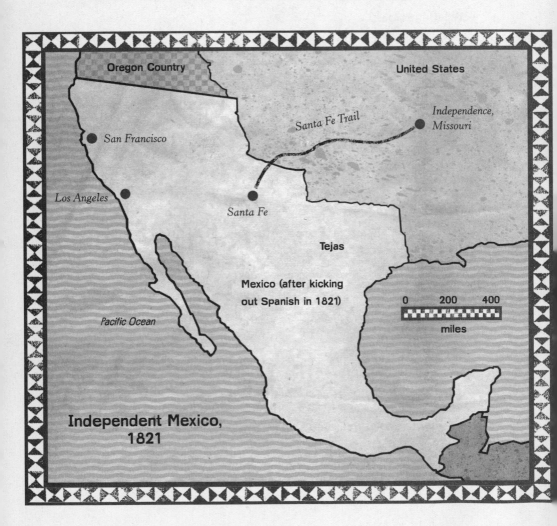

Look at that large area in northern Mexico marked *Tejas,* or Texas, as Americans called it. Very few people lived there, and the Mexican government was looking for settlers. So they were pleased when a twenty-nine-year-old man from Missouri named Stephen Austin led about three hundred American families to Texas in 1822.

Stories about sunny Texas soon spread. You could buy huge chunks of good land for a small fraction of the price of farmland in the United States. Thousands of Americans packed up their stuff and scratched "G.T.T." on the doors of their cabins. Everyone knew what that meant: "Gone to Texas."

Settlers in Texas were supposed to promise loyalty to the Mexican government and obey Mexican laws, including a ban on slavery. But the Mexican capital, Mexico City, was 1,200 miles to the south. Mexican officials simply had no way of controlling what people did in Texas. As a result, American settlers basically governed themselves. They liked it that way.

By 1830 there were more than 20,000 Americans in Texas. This was beginning to worry Mexican leaders—they felt they were losing control of their land to the Americans (or, as they called them, *"los Yanquis"*). The Mexican president, Antonio López de Santa Anna, decided to get tough with the Americans. He declared he would cut immigration, collect taxes, and enforce Mexican law. And he'd use force to do it, if necessary.

But by now Texans were used to independence. They reacted angrily to Santa Anna's threats. "Every man in Texas is called upon to take up arms in defense of his country and his rights," declared Stephen Austin.

True, Texans weren't actually in their country. But they felt like it was their home. They were ready to fight for it.

Step 12: Meet Me in San Antonio

In 1835 Santa Anna sent his brother-in-law to Texas to teach the Americans a lesson by seizing control of the town of San Antonio. The brother-in-law didn't really know how to seize towns. He ended up surrendering San Antonio to the Texans.

Now Santa Anna was furious. Pronouncing himself a military genius (he called himself "the Napoleon of the West"), Santa Anna vowed to personally crush the rebels.

"The great problem I had to solve was to reconquer Texas and to accomplish this in the shortest time possible."

He even threatened to march all the way to the White House while he was at it. But first things first: Santa Anna headed toward Texas, his personal wagons loaded with silverware, china plates, and a silver chamber pot. He seemed less worried about the comfort of his

Antonio López de Santa Anna

four thousand soldiers. Short on food, tents, and medicine, many of the men starved or froze to death in blizzards as the army stumbled north.

In San Antonio, meanwhile, Texas soldiers gathered in an old Spanish mission known as the Alamo. This was a crumbling church, with a courtyard of about two and a half acres, all surrounded by tall stone walls.

When Santa Anna and his soldiers finally made it to San Antonio in February 1836, they quickly surrounded the Alamo. Trapped inside were about 180 volunteer soldiers, both Americans and Tejanos, or Mexicans from Texas. Many of the soldiers' families were stuck in there too.

William Travis, one of the leaders of the Texas army, dashed off a desperate note addressed "To the People of Texas & All Americans in the World":

"FELLOW CITIZENS AND COMPATRIOTS—I am

besieged, by a thousand or more Mexicans under Santa Anna. . . .

The enemy has demanded a surrender. . . . I have answered the

demand with a cannon shot, and our flag still waves proudly from

the walls—I shall never surrender or retreat."

Just a few days later, before sunrise on the chilly morning of March 6, a Texan named John Baugh looked over the walls and saw Mexican soldiers charging toward the Alamo.

Baugh broke the morning silence with the shout: "Colonel Travis! The Mexicans are coming!"

Did Someone Say "Manifest Destiny"?

Eight-year-old Enrique Esparza was sleeping in a small room in the church at the Alamo. He was jolted awake by a blast of gunfire. "It was so dark that we couldn't see anything," he remembered.

"Gregorio, the soldiers have jumped the wall," Enrique's mother said to his father. "The fight's begun."

Enrique watched his father get up, grab his gun, and run out to join the battle. "I never saw him again," Enrique said.

Remember the Alamo!

Enrique and his mother, and about fifteen other women and children, huddled in the corners of the room as the battle for the Alamo grew louder. "We could hear the Mexican officers shouting to the men," Enrique said, "and the men were fighting so close that we could hear them strike each other."

Susanna Dickinson was in a nearby room, clutching her baby daughter, wondering how the fight was going. "The struggle lasted more than two hours when my husband rushed into the church where I was with my child," she said.

"Great God, Sue, the Mexicans are inside our walls!" shouted Almeron Dickinson. "All is lost! If they spare you, save my child."

Almeron was right—all was lost. By 6:30 that morning, the badly outnumbered Texans were forced to surrender. Santa Anna's soldiers killed all 183 Texas soldiers—stabbing many of them with bayonets after they had surrendered.

Later that March, Mexican soldiers defeated another small American army near the town of Goliad, Texas. About four hundred Americans were taken prisoner. Following Santa Anna's orders, Mexican soldiers marched the prisoners to an open field, shot and bayoneted all of them, and set the bodies on fire.

Enraged Texans promised payback. As one young soldier in the Texas army explained: "The boys were continually talking about the butchery at the Alamo and the slaughter at Goliad; and vowing to avenge the cold-blooded murder of their countrymen."

Revenge at San Jacinto

The job of getting revenge belonged to the volunteers of the Texas army—about eight hundred men under the command of Sam Houston. Some doubted that Houston was the right man for the job. While serving as governor of Tennessee a few years back, he had quit suddenly, refusing to give a reason. He had gone to live with the Cherokees, who soon nicknamed him "Big Drunk" (he was six foot two, and often drunk).

On the plus side, Houston had the ability to remain cool under pressure. And he had a good plan. He began retreating east across Texas, forcing Santa Anna's larger army to chase him two hundred miles. All the while, he watched and waited for the perfect moment to turn and strike.

Houston saw his opportunity near the San Jacinto River on April 21, 1836. "Let us fight fast and hard," he told his men. "We must win or die." The Texans charged forward shouting, "Remember the Alamo! Remember Goliad!"

Sam Houston

The attack surprised the entire Mexican army, especially its commander. "I was in a deep sleep when I was awakened by the firing and noise," confessed Santa Anna. He jumped up from his nap, put on his red slippers, stepped out of his tent—and immediately burst into a panic.

"I saw His Excellency running about in the utmost excitement, wringing his hands, and unable to give an order," recalled a Mexican officer.

The Texans won the battle in just eighteen minutes. And they did remember the Alamo and Goliad—maybe too well. It took Houston's officers a while to get the Texans to stop killing Mexican soldiers. When it was all over, nearly six hundred Mexicans were dead, compared with only nine Texans.

Texas soldiers caught Santa Anna (he was trying to escape disguised as a Mexican private), and the Mexican leader agreed to pull his troops out of Texas. So that was that—Texas had its independence. Some Texans were hoping to join the United States, but for now Texas was an independent country. We'll keep an eye on the situation.

Meanwhile, since we're speaking of land that was not yet part of the United States . . .

Honeymoon in Oregon

It was a busy week for Narcissa Prentiss. This young school-teacher from a small New York town got married on February 18, 1836. The next day, she and her husband, Marcus Whitman, set out for their new home in the Oregon Country—on the other side of the continent.

The Oregon Country (the area that now makes up Oregon, Washington, and Idaho) was a huge section of land claimed by both Great Britain and the United States. Both basically said, *I saw it first!* But aside from a few mountain men, no one from Britain or the United States was actually living there. The Whitmans were about to help change that. Their plan was to settle in Oregon and work as missionaries, teaching Christianity to the Walla Walla, Spokane, Nez Perce, and other Native Americans of the region.

In her journal Narcissa called the trip to Oregon "an unheard of journey for females." She was right. No American woman had ever made this 2,400-mile trek across the Great Plains and over the Rocky Mountains.

As if it were not going to be difficult enough, Narcissa found out at the last second that she and her husband would be traveling with two other missionaries: Henry Spalding and his new wife, Eliza. Henry had asked Narcissa to marry him a few years before, and she had turned him down. He was still bitter about it. So Narcissa knew there would be some awkward moments as the two couples shared a tent for months on their way west.

Luckily, the challenges of the trip kept everyone pretty busy. Buzzing clouds of mosquitoes and fleas surrounded the couples as their wagons bounced across the plains. There were no trees, which meant no shade from the burning sun, and no wood to make fires. In a letter to her sister, Harriet, and brother, Edward, Narcissa explained how they managed to cook:

Narcissa Whitman

"Our fuel for cooking . . . has been dried buffalo dung. We now find plenty of it and it answers a very good purpose, similar to the kind of coal used in Pennsylvania. I suppose Harriet will make a face at this, but if she was here she would be glad to have her supper cooked at any rate."

Their food was mainly buffalo meat, which everyone got sick of after a few weeks. "I thought of Mother's bread and butter many times," Narcissa wrote. The only really dangerous moment came when Eliza's horse took a wrong step. "Yesterday my horse became unmanageable in consequence of stepping into a hornets' nest," Eliza explained. She was thrown from the horse, but that wasn't the worst part. "My foot remained a moment in the stirrup, and my body dragged some distance," she said.

You had to be tough to cross the continent, and Eliza obviously was—she was back on the trail the next day.

After six long months of traveling, the Whitmans and Spaldings reached the Oregon Country. We'll check back with them later. For now, the important thing to know is that their journey helped show Americans that women and families could travel safely to Oregon. The route they had taken became known as the Oregon Trail. And over the next few years, thousands of families set out on the trail, hoping to claim a piece of rich Oregon farmland.

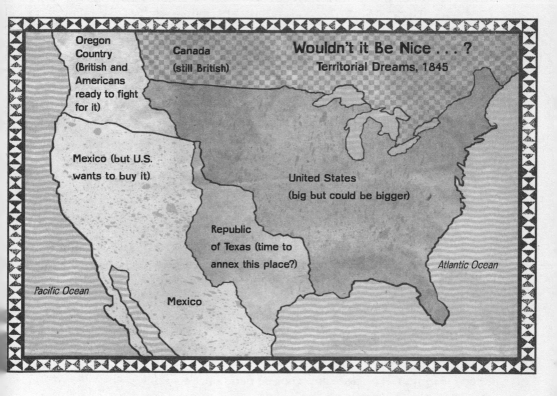

Oregon Country (British and Americans ready to fight for it)

Canada (still British)

Wouldn't it Be Nice . . . ?
Territorial Dreams, 1845

Mexico (but U.S. wants to buy it)

United States (big but could be bigger)

Republic of Texas (time to annex this place?)

Atlantic Ocean

Pacific Ocean

Mexico

Manifest Destiny Declared

By 1840 Americans knew about the Rocky Mountains from mountain men and had heard all about New Mexico from traveling merchants. Settlers in Texas and Oregon sent back letters describing land that was fertile and cheap. Many Americans began to think, *Wouldn't it be nice if all that land were ours?*

Lots of them believed it should be. Some were convinced that God wanted it that way—that it was God's plan to have the American style of democracy spread across the continent to the Pacific Ocean. This idea was summed up by the journalist John O'Sullivan: "The American claim is by the right of our manifest destiny to overspread and to possess the whole of the continent which Providence has given us for the development of the great experiment of liberty."

The phrase *manifest destiny* soon became famous (*manifest* means "clear to see" or "obvious"). O'Sullivan was saying that it was clearly the destiny of the United States to spread from the Atlantic to the Pacific. Was he right? James K. Polk thought so.

"Who Is James K. Polk?"

When leaders of the Democratic Party met to choose a presidential candidate in 1844, they couldn't agree on anyone they really liked. So they decided to compromise on someone they sort of liked—a former Tennessee governor named James K. Polk.

The leaders of the Whig Party—the other major political party in the United States at that time—were thrilled to be running against this guy. The Whigs' campaign motto was "Who is James K. Polk?"

He may not have been too famous, but Polk was very clear about what he would do if elected. A strong believer in manifest destiny, Polk insisted that the United States should immediately annex Texas (make it part of the United States, in other words). *Then,* he said, *we should force Great Britain to give up its claims to Oregon. Then we'll buy the rest of the West from Mexico.*

These popular ideas helped Polk win a close election (at forty-nine, he was the youngest president to be elected up to that point). He took over as president in March 1845, getting right to work on his plans to expand the United States. In fact, he worked so quickly that in just a few days he nearly started two wars.

First the United States annexed Texas, which brought cheers from Texas and howls of anger from the Mexican capital.

James K. Polk?

Many Mexicans still thought of Texas as part of their country, and they considered the American annexation a cause for war.

British leaders, meanwhile, refused Polk's demands that they give up claims to Oregon. The British government started making threats and preparing to fight.

Polk's reply? He was ready to fight both countries at once.

35

Exploring with the Blockheads

But even the threat of war didn't stop Americans from heading west. If it was the United States' manifest destiny to own the West, American leaders figured they might as well find out what was there. Up to that point, there were no accurate maps of most of the West. The powerful senator Thomas Hart Benton gave the job of making new maps to a young man named John Frémont (whose main qualification for mapping the West was that he was Benton's son-in-law).

Frémont put together a team of explorers, including a German mapmaker named Charles Preuss. Preuss was not what you would call an outdoorsman. The moment the crew set out from St. Louis, he began whining about the aches in his body from riding on horses and sleeping on hard ground. Some of his early journal entries tell of other complaints:

"Weather good. Food bad."

"I wish I were in Washington with my old girl."

"I wish I had a drink."

When the men killed an ox for food, Preuss wrote these entries in his journal:

June 12: *Some of the men tried to eat the liver raw. I was satisfied with bread and coffee; I am not yet so hungry that I would gulp down very fresh meat, which is repulsive to me. Tomorrow, to be sure, it will taste excellent.*

June 13: *It did not taste excellent.*

And speaking of food, Preuss noted, when they did get some decent meat, the cook always ruined it. "That fool had packed neither sugar nor salt nor pepper," wrote Pruess. "What good is the best food stuff if one cannot prepare it properly?"

As they headed farther west that summer, it got unbearably hot and buggy. Then there were endless and exhausting climbs into the Rocky Mountains. "No supper, no breakfast, little or no sleep," Preuss wrote. "Who can enjoy climbing a mountain under these circumstances?"

He was particularly annoyed that Frémont kept stopping to collect samples of rocks and plants. "That fellow knows nothing about mineralogy or botany," wrote Preuss. "Yet he collects every trifle. . . . Let him collect as much as he wants—if he would only not make us wait for our meal. . . . Oh, you American blockheads!"

Preuss's only kind words were for a small group of Indians who saved him when he got lost in the desert and was dying of hunger. "I walked straight up to them, sat down among them, and gave them to understand that I was hungry," he wrote. "They immediately served me acorns, some of which I ate, and others I put in my pocket. When they saw this, they themselves filled both my pockets."

He may have been miserable, but Preuss was a very good mapmaker (and he needed the job to support his family). Suffering through three long journeys across the West in the 1840s, Preuss produced the most accurate maps yet of the region. The maps were published along with Frémont's journals—which Frémont's wife, Jesse, rewrote for him when he got home.

These maps and journals became huge best sellers. They got Americans even more interested in all that land to the west.

Oregon Fever Rages

The idea of moving to Oregon was especially exciting. "The Oregon fever is raging in almost every part of the union," reported one newspaper.

It was hard for easterners to resist the fever when they heard tales of Oregon's mild climate and fertile soil. One farmer listened to a land promoter trying to persuade people to move to Oregon:

"They do say, gentlemen, they do say that out in Oregon the pigs are running about under the great acorn trees, round and fat, and already cooked, with knives and forks sticking in them so that you can cut off a slice whenever you are hungry."

No one really believed that (let's hope), but thousands of families were convinced that they could build a better life in Oregon. Actually, by reading diaries from that time, we see that it was almost always the husbands who made the decision to move west. Wives were often more reluctant to leave their friends and family behind, knowing they would probably never see each other again. "Dr. Wilson has determined to go," wrote a young woman named Margaret Wilson. "I am going with him, as there is no other alternative."

Once the decision was made, the next step was to pack up a wagon and head to Missouri, where the Oregon Trail began. There you could stock up on important supplies like flour, bacon, sugar, coffee, and barrels of water. And you could team up with other families and hire a guide, usually an out-of-work mountain man. Mountain men had killed off most of the beavers in the West, but now they found new careers guiding families along the Oregon Trail.

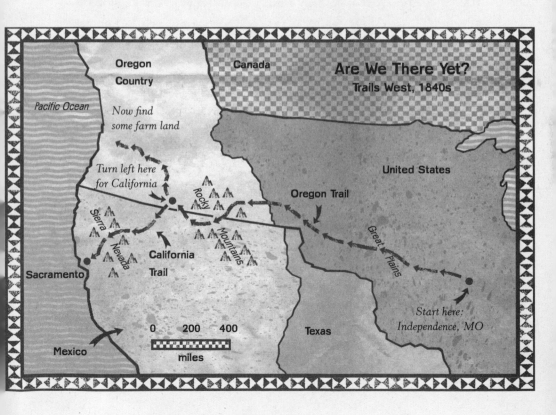

Are We There Yet?
Trails West, 1840s

Oregon Country

Canada

Pacific Ocean

Now find some farm land

Turn left here for California

United States

Rocky Mountains

Oregon Trail

Sierra Nevada

California Trail

Great Plains

Sacramento

Start here: Independence, MO

0   200   400
miles

Texas

Mexico

Are We There Yet?

Even with an expert guide, this was an exhausting and dangerous 2,400-mile trip. Dragged forward by oxen, wagons rocked along at a top speed of two miles an hour. Men kept busy herding the families' farm animals, repairing the wagons, and hunting for dinner. Women worked even harder, getting up at four a.m. to start breakfast, then working all day and late into the night—cooking, cleaning, washing and mending clothes, taking care of young children . . .

Bigger kids walked alongside the wagon, lightening the load a little for the poor oxen. As they walked, children had the key job of collecting buffalo chips, which were used for cooking fuel. The chips burned quickly, so they had to gather huge piles of them for every meal.

Once they were out on what seemed like the endless Great Plains, many families started wishing they had packed a bit lighter. They wondered, *Do we really need this heavy kitchen table? Wouldn't we move a bit faster without these extra chairs?* Desperate to speed up their journey, they started tossing stuff out the backs of their wagons, littering the road to Oregon with a trail of furniture, mirrors, tools, stoves, beds, and clothing.

Aside from simply being sick of traveling, families had another reason for wanting to move quickly. "During the entire trip Indians were a source of anxiety, we being never sure of their friendship," explained one traveler. It was a relief to discover that Native Americans were much more interested in trading with travelers than attacking them. The two main causes of death for early Oregon Trail travelers might surprise you. Number one: gun accidents. Number two: drowning while trying to cross rivers.

As more and more travelers crowded the trail, a new problem became clear—to both eyes and noses. The route was dotted with countless mounds of human waste. "The stench is sometimes almost unendurable," said a traveler named Charlotte Pengra. These stinky piles polluted water supplies, helping to spread deadly diseases. Disease soon became the deadliest danger on the Oregon Trail. Just ask Catherine Sager.

The Sad Sager Saga

Catherine Sager was nine years old when she and her father, pregnant mother, and five brothers and sisters set out on the Oregon Trail in the spring of 1844. Soon after starting, her mother gave birth to a baby girl. Then they got right back on the road.

Catherine was expecting a tough journey, but she was surprised by the first major problem the family faced: seasickness. "The motion of the wagon made us all sick," she remembered. "It was weeks before we got used to the seasick motion."

Once they got used to the bouncing, the Sager kids came up with travel games, like jumping in and out of the wagon while it was moving. It was lots of fun—until one day in August:

"When performing this feat that afternoon my dress caught . . . and I was thrown under the wagon wheels, both of which passed over me, badly crushing the left leg, before father could stop the oxen."

Catherine Sager

Catherine's father leaped down and scooped up his daughter. "My dear child," he cried, "your leg is broken all to pieces!" A doctor from another wagon put her leg in a cast. Then they got right back on the road.

From then on Catherine rode in the wagon, or walked alongside on crutches (that shows you how slow the oxen were—she could keep up on crutches!). Anyway, this turned out to be the good part of the trip. Catherine's father soon caught a fever, grew weaker and weaker, and died. He was buried along the trail. Less than a month later, her mother got sick (she had never fully recovered from a difficult childbirth). She died and was also buried by the trail.

"So in twenty-six days we became orphans," Catherine wrote. "Seven children of us, the oldest fourteen and the youngest a babe." Too far west to turn back, they had no choice but to get back in their wagon and continue on to Oregon. Other families on the trail helped the Sager children prepare food and take care of their baby sister. All seven Sager kids made it to Oregon, where they were dropped off at the home of Narcissa and Marcus Whitman—the missionaries who had traveled to Oregon almost ten years before.

"She spoke kindly to us as she came up," Catherine said of her first meeting with Narcissa Whitman. "But like frightened things we ran behind the cart, peeping shyly around at her."

Whitman asked the boys why they were crying. They told her.

"Poor boys, no wonder you weep!" she said.

The Whitmans took in all seven Sagers. The children found Narcissa Whitman kind and generous, though very strict. Catherine's sister Matilda explained how Narcissa ran her house: "She would point to one of us, then point to the dishes or the broom, and we would instantly get busy."

Which Way to California?

Americans continued moving west for all the usual reasons—the desire for land, the hunger for adventure, the need to find work or escape debt. A twenty-one-year-old teacher named John Bidwell had a slightly stranger motive. When he came home to his Missouri farm after summer vacation, some other guy was living there! The guy claimed the farm was his now—and did so while pointing a shotgun at Bidwell's chest.

That's when Bidwell decided to move west.

He knew about Oregon, of course, but he had also heard interesting stories of California, a vast land of mountains and grassy valleys in northern Mexico. There was only one problem. "Our ignorance of the route was complete," Bidwell confessed. "We knew that California lay west, and that was the extent of our knowledge."

He was right about the west part. California stretched along the western coast of North America for eight hundred miles. Growing up in California in the early 1800s, Guadalupe Vallejo spent his childhood riding the open spaces between ranches and towns. "We traveled as much as possible on horseback," he said. "Every one seemed to live outdoors."

"We were the pioneers of the Pacific coast, building towns and missions while General Washington was carrying on the war of the Revolution."

Guadalupe Vallejo

Vallejo's history was correct: the Spanish had founded San Diego, Los Angeles, and San Francisco in the late 1700s. Vallejo lived near San Francisco Bay, enjoying parties, dances, feasts, bullfights, and rodeos. He even liked the grizzly bears. "The young Spanish gentlemen often rode out on moonlit nights to lasso these bears," Vallejo said, "and then they would drag them through the village street, and past the houses of their friends."

Of course, there's always another side to the story. The reason Spanish families had so much time for fun was that they forced Native Americans to do most of the hard work of running ranches and farms.

By the 1840s California was home to about 7,000 Spanish settlers and 150,000 Native Americans—and a growing number of Americans. The American teacher John Bidwell made it to California, barely surviving tornadoes and hailstorms, flooding rivers, and torturous thirst. (At one point in the desert, the only water he could find was so muddy and smelly, he had to brew it into coffee before his horses would drink it.)

Bidwell's route to California became known as the California Trail. And as Americans started traveling this trail, they found all the dreaded dangers of the Oregon Trail, with one bonus danger: the Sierra Nevada mountain range.

Beware of Shortcuts

The snow starts falling early in the Sierra Nevada, so it was absolutely essential for travelers to get up and over these rugged mountains by October.

With this in mind, a businessman named John Hastings started selling a guide to the California Trail in 1845. In the book he described a shortcut that would allow travelers to reach the Sierra Nevada more quickly. The so-called Hastings Cutoff really was shorter. Unfortunately for travelers, Hastings failed to mention the massive deserts and canyons and mountains along his recommended route—possibly because he had never actually seen the route. He just wanted to make it sound easy to get to California so people would come there and buy stuff from his stores.

A year after Hastings's guide was published, a group of about eighty travelers led by the Donner and Reed families read the book. "Hastings's cutoff is said to be a savings of 350 or 400 miles, and a better route," said James Reed.

He and his friends decided to give it a try.

"I was a child when we started to California," said James Reed's daughter Virginia, who was twelve when the trip began. "Yet I remember the journey well and I have cause to remember it."

The Donner Party, as they became known, left the established trail in August, heading into the deserts west of the Great Salt Lake. With only Hastings's inaccurate maps to guide them, the group was soon lost and dangerously low on water. They lightened their wagons by tossing belongings out onto the baking sand. Their oxen started dying anyway.

Growing increasingly tense and desperate, some of the men started fighting. A man named John Snyder attacked James Reed with a whip. Reed stabbed Snyder, killing him. Though Reed had acted in self-defense, the other men voted to kick Reed out of the group. He was sent off into the desert without food or weapons.

"When we learned of this decision, I followed him through the darkness . . . and carried him his rifle, pistols, ammunition, and some food. I had determined to stay with him, and begged him to let me stay, but he would listen to no argument, saying that it was impossible."

Virginia was crying so hard, she could barely walk back to camp. When she got there, she saw the fear in the eyes of her mother and younger sister and brothers. "It seemed suddenly to make a woman of me," she said. "I realized that I must be strong."

Virginia Reed

You Call This a Party?

The Donner Party continued west, beginning their climb into the Sierra Nevada in late October. Snow flurries were already starting.

"The farther we went up, the deeper the snow got," Virginia said. "The wagons could not go."

By early November the whole group was stuck in snowdrifts high in the mountains. They built tiny wooden cabins, and killed and ate the last of their animals. Every day the snow piled higher: ten feet, then twenty, then twenty-five. And months of winter still lay ahead.

Facing certain starvation, fifteen of the strongest members of the party (ten men and five women) decided to try to make it out of the mountains and send back help. They took enough food for six days.

Nine days later they were hopelessly lost in the snowy peaks. As the men and women huddled together around a tiny fire, someone brought up the awful question on everyone's mind: Should they kill and eat one member of the group in order to save the others? "Even the wind seemed to hold its breath as the suggestion was made that were one to die, the rest might live," Virginia wrote. "Then the suggestion was made that lots be cast and whoever drew the longest slip should be the sacrifice."

No one had the heart to go through with the plan. But when several group members died of cold and starvation over the next few nights, the others did the only thing they could to survive: they cut flesh from the bodies, roasted it, and ate it. Then they packed up the extra meat (carefully labeling the pieces, so no one would eat his or her own family member) and continued the journey. Seven of them (two of the men and all five of the women) made it out of the mountains alive, reaching settlements in California.

As news of the Donner Party spread, volunteer rescue crews rushed into the mountains to try to save the people still stuck there. A volunteer named Daniel Rhoads found the spot where the Donner Party cabins were supposed to be. He saw no sign of the buildings. Then he realized he was standing on them—the cabins had been completely buried by snow.

"We saw a woman emerge from a hole in the snow," Rhoads reported. "As we approached her, several others made their appearance, in like manner coming out of the snow."

One of the women, barely more than a skeleton, said in a shaky voice: "Are you men from California or do you come from heaven?"

Other rescue teams soon arrived, including one led by Virginia Reed's father, James (who had found his way to California on his own). Of the eighty-six members of the Donner Party, forty-one died before the last survivors were rescued in April 1847. Amazingly, Virginia's entire family survived. More amazingly, Virginia seemed to quickly put the winter's horrors behind her. "We are all very well pleased with California," she wrote to a cousin that spring. "It is a beautiful country. It ought to be a beautiful country to pay us for our trouble getting there."

She added this advice for anyone thinking of coming to California: "Remember, never take no cutoffs and hurry along as fast as you can."

Now Back to Polk

President James K. Polk wasn't thinking of going to California. He was thinking about how to make it part of the United States.

Remember, Polk had run for president on the promise of expanding American territory. Last we heard, Polk was threatening to fight Great Britain over Oregon and Mexico over the rest of the West.

The Oregon conflict turned out to be pretty easy to resolve. After lots of tough talk, Britain and the United States agreed to simply split the territory. In June 1846 the United States officially took over the huge chunk of land that is now the northwest region of the country.

The conflict with Mexico was much more dangerous. Furious Mexican leaders had two major complaints. One, the United States had no right to annex Texas, they argued. Two, even if the United States did annex Texas, Americans were grabbing too much land. The Mexicans insisted that the Nueces River formed the southern border of Texas. Everything south of the river was not part of Texas—so it was still Mexican territory, annexation or no annexation.

Polk saw it differently. He argued that the border of Texas was actually 150 miles farther south, at the Rio Grande—so all that extra land came with Texas.

With this border dispute raging, Polk offered to buy New Mexico and California from Mexico. It probably wasn't the right time to ask. In no mood to lose even more land to the Americans, offended Mexican leaders angrily rejected Polk's offer.

Then Polk cranked the tension up another notch. In March 1846 he sent American soldiers to Texas. Under Polk's orders, the troops crossed the Nueces River and continued south into the land claimed by both the United States and Mexico. The soldiers were there to defend American territory, Polk explained.

But to Mexican officials, this was an invasion of the Mexican state of Tamaulipas. General Pedro de Ampudia warned the Americans:

"If you insist on remaining upon the soil of the Department of Tamaulipas, it will certainly result that arms, and arms alone, must decide the question."

General Zachary Taylor, commander of the American troops, assured the Mexicans that he did insist on remaining. By April the two armies were glaring at each other across the one-hundred-yard-wide Rio Grande.

Both sides expected an explosion of violence at any moment.

Pedro de Ampudia

War, Land, Gold, Trouble

On April 25, 1846, Mexican soldiers splashed across the Rio Grande and attacked a small group of American troops. Sixteen Americans were killed, and the rest captured. "Hostilities have commenced," General Taylor wrote to President Polk. When the letter reached Washington (it took a couple of weeks), Polk immediately went to Congress to demand a declaration of war: "Mexico has passed the boundary of the United States," he said, "has invaded our territory and shed American blood upon the American soil."

Cause for War?

Had the shooting really started in American territory? Some members of Congress didn't think so. "That soil was not ours," said a little-known House member from Illinois named Abraham Lincoln. To Lincoln, it looked like Polk had purposely sent Americans soldiers into the disputed territory in order to spark a war with Mexico. The war would give the United States an excuse to capture the land Mexico had refused to sell. *Pretty rotten,* thought Senator Alexander Stephens of Georgia: "The principle of waging war against a neighboring people to compel them to sell their country, is not only dishonorable, but disgraceful."

Polk objected, pointing out that Mexico had started the shooting. He had always wanted peace with Mexico, he insisted. His opponents joked that what Polk really wanted was not peace *with* Mexico, but a piece *of* Mexico.

Either way, the public was on Polk's side. American soldiers had been attacked, and there was strong support for war. Congress voted to declare war on Mexico in May 1846. Thousands of Americans rushed to volunteer for military service.

As for Abraham Lincoln, he soon heard from angry voters back home, who said his opposition to the war was pretty much an act of treason. One Illinois newspaper actually called him "a second Benedict Arnold." That was the end of Lincoln's political career, experts said.

Santa Anna Does It Again

"**M**exico should fight to the end," declared a newspaper in the Mexican city of Nuevo Leon. "As long as there is one man remaining, he should go and fight the unjust invaders."

The problem with this plan: the Mexican army was in awful shape. Most Mexican soldiers had very little training and terrible equipment, including old-fashioned muskets sold to them by the British (left over from wars Britain had fought thirty years ago). The army could not even have survived without *soldaderas*, women who traveled along with the troops and did work the army should have done: cooking, making uniforms, caring for the sick and wounded.

Another serious problem was that the Mexican army was led by General Antonio López de Santa Anna, the self-proclaimed genius who had lost Texas. Santa Anna was good at talking tough, not so good at actual fighting. When his army faced Americans at the Battle of Buena Vista in early 1847, Santa Anna demanded that the Americans surrender in order to save themselves.

"Tell Santa Anna to go to [censored]!" barked Zachary Taylor. Then Taylor turned to a staff member and said: "Major Bliss, put that in Spanish, and send it back."

Bliss put Taylor's main idea into slightly more polite language: "I beg leave to say that I decline acceding to your request."

Santa Anna attacked, lost five times more

men than the Americans, and declared victory. Then he retreated. In a series of short, brutal battles in the spring and summer of 1847, the American army continued slashing its way toward Mexico City.

Meanwhile, the war with Mexico gave Polk an excuse to do something he'd wanted to do anyway—send American troops to capture California.

Is That Supposed to Be a Bear?

Mariano Guadalupe Vallejo woke suddenly on the morning of June 14, 1846, startled by the sounds of shouts and horses. "I looked out of my bedroom window," Vallejo said. "To my great surprise, I made out groups of armed men scattered to the right and left of my residence."

As Mexico's military commander in northern California (and uncle to the young pioneer on page 44), Vallejo had always been welcoming to American immigrants. He often invited newcomers to stay at his large ranch in Sonoma and helped them settle in California. But that did him no good when armed Americans banged on his door.

"My wife advised me to try and flee by the rear door," Vallejo remembered. "But I told her that such a step was unworthy and that under no circumstances could I decide to desert my young family at such a critical time." He jumped into his general's uniform and opened his door. "The house was immediately filled with armed men," he said.

These weren't Polk's soldiers—just regular guys with guns, wearing greasy clothes and very dirty hats. "They were about as rough-looking a set of men as one could well imagine," admitted Robert Semple, one of the Americans.

Too polite to say what he was really thinking, Vallejo asked, "To what happy circumstances shall I attribute the visit of so many exalted personages?"

Shouting all at once, the Americans declared that they were there to arrest Vallejo. They were seizing California from Mexico! (And while they were at it, they seized Vallejo's brandy, and downed it in quick gulps.)

Then the Americans marched to the town plaza in Sonoma, declared California to be an independent republic, and raised a homemade flag on which they had painted a grizzly bear. Well, it was supposed to be a bear.

"The bear was so badly painted," Vallejo said, "it looked more like a pig than a bear."

Anyway, the key point is that these Americans had heard that the United States was at war with Mexico. They decided it was a good time to seize California for their country.

A few weeks later, the American soldiers and sailors sent by President Polk started arriving. They took control of California for the United States.

Redraw the Map Again

In September 1847 American soldiers captured Mexico City. Having lost the war, Mexican leaders were forced to accept the same basic deal they had angrily rejected two years before. In the Treaty of Guadalupe Hidalgo, Mexico gave up nearly half its territory, including the disputed land in Texas, all of California, New Mexico, and the rest of what is now the southwestern United States. The United States paid Mexico fifteen million dollars.

Now the West is West:
U.S. in 1848

Oregon Territory
(treaty with
Britain, 1846)

Land gained from Mexico
(Treaty of Guadalupe
Hidalgo, 1848)

We already had all of this.

Texas
(annexed in 1845)

bought from Mexico
in 1853

Now all the land we think of as the West today was part of the United States.

More Settlers

While all this was going on, more and more Americans were showing up in the West. Followers of the new Mormon religion even established their own western trail. After getting violently chased out of towns in Missouri and Illinois, the Mormons were looking for a new place to settle. The Mormon leader Brigham Young read about the Great Salt Lake Valley—a giant salty lake surrounded by deserts. It sounded like a good place to be left alone.

In the spring of 1847, Young and his followers established the Mormon Trail, a 1,300-mile route from Illinois to what is now Utah. When the travelers arrived in the Salt Lake Valley, they were not impressed. "A paradise of the lizard, the cricket, and the rattlesnake," one settler said. That was fine by Brigham Young.

"I want hard times, so that every person that does not wish to stay for the sake of his religion will leave."

Brigham Young

The Mormon settlers began irrigating fields, planting crops, building homes, and laying out the streets of a new town. It took them just a few years to turn Salt Lake City into the second-largest city west of Missouri (only San Francisco was bigger).

And More Trouble

Meanwhile, thousands of other Americans were heading west, most of them on the Oregon Trail. When they arrived in Oregon, many travelers stopped to rest at the home of Narcissa and Marcus Whitman—remember them? They're the missionaries who had settled in Oregon and taken in the orphaned Sager children.

The Cayuse and other Indians of the region watched this migration with growing alarm. Ten years before, Cayuse leaders had invited the Whitmans to settle on their land. The Whitmans told them they were there to teach and help the local people. But now the Whitmans were using their house as a welcome station for huge groups of white settlers. This was not at all what the Cayuse had agreed to. "The poor Indians are amazed at the overwhelming numbers of Americans coming into the country," Narcissa Whitman wrote.

They had good reason to be amazed, and angry too. The new settlers not only grabbed big chunks of land, but they also brought diseases that had not existed in that part of the world. Measles, for example, was not very dangerous for people of European background. They had developed natural defenses to it over many centuries. But when American settlers brought measles to Oregon in 1847, the disease quickly killed half the people in many Cayuse villages—and nearly all of the children.

Unable to escape from this nightmare, some Cayuse began

wondering, *How come Marcus Whitman, who is a doctor, is able to cure most of the white children, while our own children continue to die?* A rumor started spreading that the Whitmans were purposely using the disease to wipe the Cayuse out.

"The disease was raging fearfully among the Indians, who were rapidly dying," said Catherine Sager. "I saw from five to six buried daily." Four years earlier Catherine had watched her parents die on the Oregon Trail. Now she was thirteen and in for another horrible shock.

The Whitman Massacre

The morning of November 29 was foggy and cold, Catherine Sager remembered. She was at home with the Whitmans, helping to care for sick children. There was a sudden burst of banging on the front door.

Outside, pounding with his fists, was a Cayuse chief named Tilou-kaikt, along with several other Cayuse men. Tiloukaikt had just seen three of his children die of measles. Now he was shouting for Dr. Whitman to let him in and give him medicine for other sick children.

Marcus Whitman let the men into the kitchen. Catherine, who was in the living room with Narcissa Whitman, heard angry yelling. "Suddenly there was a sharp explosion," she said, "a rifle shot in the kitchen, and we all jumped in fright."

Moments later a girl named Mary Ann stumbled into the room.

"Did they kill the doctor?" Narcissa cried.

Panting and pale with shock, Mary Ann managed to say "Yes."

"My husband is killed and I am left a widow!" wailed Narcissa.

Through the living room window, Catherine could see Cayuse men attacking other settlers in nearby buildings. "Then a bullet came through the window, piercing Mrs. Whitman's shoulder," Catherine said. "Clasping her hands to the wound, she shrieked with pain, and then fell to the floor. I ran to her and tried to raise her up."

"Child, you cannot help me, save yourself," Narcissa told Catherine.

Catherine helped carry her younger sisters and two other girls up to the attic, where they hid until dark. Several of the girls were sick with measles, and they called out desperately for water. Catherine could not help them. Finally they passed out from exhaustion. The attic grew quiet.

"I sat upon the side of the bed," said Catherine, "watching hour after hour, while the horrors of the day passed and re-passed before my mind." She heard the clock downstairs strike ten, then eleven, then midnight. She listened to the steady breathing of the sleeping children, and the sounds of cats' paws on the floor downstairs.

Catherine and her sisters survived that terrible night. But Tiloukaikt and his men had killed the Whitmans and eleven other settlers, including two of Catherine's brothers. Calling for vengeance, white settlers formed armed groups and attacked Cayuse villages, killing many people who had nothing to do with the crime. Tiloukaikt finally turned himself in. He and four other Cayuse men were tried for murder, found guilty, and hanged.

Between the measles epidemic and the attacks following the Whitman massacre, the Cayuse were nearly destroyed. Survivors went to live with other Native American groups.

And Catherine Sager was an orphan again. She and her sisters split up, moving in with different families in the Oregon Territory.

A Bloody Preview?

Violent clashes like those between the Cayuse and white settlers in Oregon didn't happen every day, of course. But the Whitman massacre is an important story because it shows how tense things could get when large numbers of settlers started moving onto Native American lands. And it shows just how quickly those tensions could explode into violence.

Can you imagine what might happen if tens of thousands of settlers suddenly raced to the West? You're about to find out.

Gold . . . Maybe

By the start of 1848, a Swiss immigrant named John Sutter had built himself a nice little empire in central California. He owned nearly 50,000 acres, including farms, orchards, stores, even his own fort—a walled complex of buildings called Sutter's Fort (soon to become part of the new town of Sacramento).

In January 1848 Sutter hired a carpenter to build a sawmill on some of his land along the American River. The carpenter, James Marshall, led a small group of workers to the spot where Sutter wanted his mill. The men unloaded their tools and started working.

On the morning of January 24, Marshall was inspecting a freshly dug hole when he stopped suddenly. "My eye was caught with the glimpse of something shining in the bottom of the ditch," he remembered. "I reached my hand down and picked it up. It made my heart thump."

Marshall held in his palm a little yellow lump, dented and creased, about half the size of a pea. He collected a few more of these lumps and showed them to William Scott, one of the workers.

Marshall: *I have found it!*

Scott: *What is it?*

Marshall: *Gold.*

Scott: *Oh! No, that can't be.*

Marshall: *I know it to be nothing else.*

Marshall was sure he had struck gold! Well, he was pretty sure. Actually,

James Marshall

he didn't really know. "It did not seem to be of the right color," he later admitted.

Only one person on Marshall's crew knew anything about gold mining—her name was Jennie Wimmer. As a teenager Wimmer had dug for gold in the streams of Georgia. Now she was working as a cook for Marshall's men. All along she had been saying that the American River looked like a promising place to search for gold. No one listened.

Now Wimmer took one of Marshall's nuggets and turned it over in her hands. It looked like yellow chewing gum, she thought, "just out of the mouth of a school girl."

She looked up and said, "This is gold."

To prove it, she dropped the nugget into a pot she was using to make lye (a chemical she needed to make soap). "I will throw it into my lye kettle . . ." she said, "and if it is gold, it will be gold when it comes out."

Wimmer knew that lye (a strong base) would quickly tarnish most metals, but would have no effect on gold. The next morning she pulled the nugget out of her kettle. "And there was the gold piece as bright as could be," she said.

The men were still not convinced.

Can You Keep a Secret?

Two days later, John Sutter was working in his office, listening to the rain pounding on his fort. He heard the door crash open and looked up. James Marshall was standing in the doorway.

"He was soaked to the skin and dripping water," Sutter recalled. "He told me he had something of the utmost importance to tell me, that he wanted to speak to me in private."

Even before that moment, Sutter had considered the excitable Marshall to be, as he put it, "like a crazy man." Now Sutter must have been really worried. But he got up and shut the door.

"Are you alone?" Marshall asked.

"Yes," said Sutter.

"Did you lock the door?"

"No, but I will if you wish it."

Marshall wished it.

Then Marshall took a rag from his pocket and unwrapped it. Sutter stepped forward and saw a few little yellow blobs.

"Well, it looks like gold," Sutter said. "Let us test it."

He got down an encyclopedia, turned to the *G* section, and looked up *gold*. He performed the tests recommended in the book, including biting the metal—pure gold is so soft that you can bite down and leave a tooth mark in it.

"I declared this to be gold of the finest quality," Sutter said.

He raced out to the American River and told his workers to keep the discovery secret. But as you've probably noticed, most people can't keep secrets. The bigger the secret, the harder it is to keep. And this was a secret that was about to change the world.

Even after swearing his workers to secrecy, Sutter himself bragged to a friend: "I have made a discovery of a gold mine, which, according to experiments we have made, is extraordinarily rich."

Then, over the first few months of 1848, Sutter's workers started showing up in San Francisco with bags of gold they had found. One worker went into a store and dropped a bag of gold flakes on the counter, announcing to everyone: "That there is gold, and I know it, and know where it comes from, and there's plenty in the same place, certain and sure!"

Recognizing a good business opportunity when he saw one, a store owner named Sam Brannan paraded through San Francisco holding up samples of the gold found by Sutter's workers and shouting, "Gold! Gold! Gold from the American River!"

As Brannan had hoped, people raced to his store to buy overpriced mining supplies. Then they rushed off to look for gold. By June 1848 three-quarters of San Francisco's population was gone. Businesses and newspapers shut down. The only school in town closed its doors (and the teacher took his students along with him to search for gold).

The Gold Fever Dance

"The whole population are going crazy," one Californian said. "Old as well as young are daily falling victim to gold fever."

A man named James Carson never forgot the moment he caught the fever. News of gold discoveries started reaching his town of Monterey, California, in the spring of 1848. He was sure the stories were exaggerated. Until . . .

"One day I saw a form, bent and filthy, approaching me," Carson remembered. "He was an old acquaintance and had been one of the first to visit the mines."

This guy had once been neat and clean. Now his clothes were ripped and his wild hair and beard sprang out in all directions. Carson watched the man open a big bag filled with yellow chunks and flakes.

"This is only what I picked out with a knife," the man told Carson.

As Carson gazed at the gold, he felt something strange happening inside him. "A frenzy seized my soul," he said. Carson was catching a disease that was about to spread across the country, across the world.

"My legs performed some entirely new movements of polka steps . . . piles of gold rose up before me at every step; castles of marble, dazzling the eye . . . in short, I had a very violent attack of the Gold Fever."

James Carson

One hour after dancing down the streets of Monterey, Carson had his mule packed with supplies and was hurrying to the gold mines.

Gold fever raced around the world, speeding through South America, Asia, Europe, even reaching the Australian island of Tasmania (eight thousand miles from California). A Tasmanian store owner started selling a new invention he called "gold grease." The idea: you take off your clothes, smear your naked body with the stuff, roll down a hill—and the gold sticks to you.

American newspapers, meanwhile, were making it sound easy to get rich in California, even without magic grease. Readers in Philadelphia opened their papers and read a letter from a California miner: "Your streams have minnows and ours are paved with gold." People all over the country were hearing similarly exciting stories.

"The gold excitement spread like wildfire, even out to our log cabin in the prairie," remembered a Missouri settler named Luzena Stanley Wilson. "And as we had almost nothing to lose, and we might gain a fortune, we early caught the fever."

Like so many Americans, the Wilson family packed up what they could carry, left everything else behind, and set out for California.

But How Do You Get There?

There was no good way to get to California. There were three bad ways.

First, you could cross the country by land, using oxen to drag your wagons along the trails to the western coast. This was bone-bruising, slow, and dangerous—and getting more dangerous all the

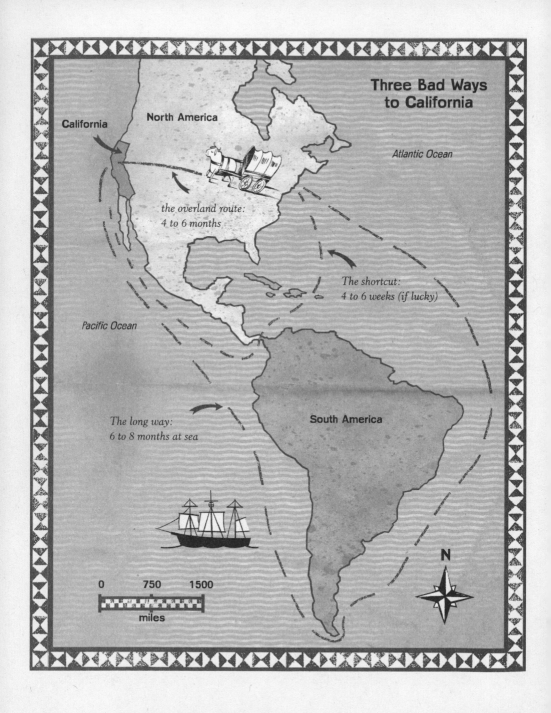

Three Bad Ways
to California

California

North America

Atlantic Ocean

the overland route:
4 to 6 months

The shortcut:
4 to 6 weeks (if lucky)

Pacific Ocean

The long way:
6 to 8 months at sea

South America

N

0   750   1500

miles

time. As the trails got busier, streams and wells along the way got more and more polluted with human waste. This led to the spread of cholera, an infection of the intestines that causes severe diarrhea and vomiting. Death was often miserable and quick, as a traveler named William Swain noted in his diary:

May 18: *One of our company, Mr. Ives, is sick with cholera.*
May 19: *Mr. Ives is dead.*

If you had about six hundred dollars to spare (which most people didn't) you could travel by sea all the way around the southern tip South America and then north to California. This was safer than the overland trails, though you had to deal with storms, seasickness, rotting food, and barrels of drinking water that got so smelly, passengers had to add molasses and vinegar before they could bear to swallow it. For many, though, the real problem with this route was that it was 15,000 miles and took six months or more—too long to wait when you've got gold fever.

The quickest route (if everything went well) was to sail to Panama, cross the seventy-five-mile-wide strip of land by canoe and on foot, and then get in another ship bound for California. Shipping company advertisements made this sound like a pleasant little shortcut. The ads failed to mention that travelers would be tripping through tropical forests and dodging disease-carrying mosquitoes.

Nor did the ads mention that when you finally stumbled into Panama City, there would probably be no ship there to pick you up. Jenny Megquier and her husband were among thousands of travelers who got stuck on Panama's Pacific coast. Every time a boat sailed

up, desperate crowds raced forward to try to get on. Megquier kept a positive attitude while waiting, though she did find some of the local bugs mildly annoying. "Another insect which is rather troublesome, gets into your feet and lays its eggs," she wrote. The doctor and I have them in our toes—did not find it out until they had deposited their eggs in large quantities; the natives dug them out and put on the ashes of tobacco."

Jenny Megquier eventually made it to California alive. So did William Swain and about 10,000 other hopeful people in 1848.

Now the Adventure Begins

Getting there was just the start of the adventure.

A young traveler named Leonard Kip realized this when his ship sailed into San Francisco's harbor. Kip woke to the sounds of the ship's captain barking curses. He found an officer and asked what was going on.

> Kip: *What's the matter?*
>
> Officer: *You will have to row yourselves ashore, as all the men have left.*
>
> Kip: *Indeed!*
>
> Officer: *Went off last night, on the sly, laughing at us on shore now—next week, in the mines.*

This was happening a lot. As soon as ships arrived in San Francisco, entire crews raced to shore and headed inland to join the gold rush. Kip looked around and saw the result: hundreds of ships gently rocking in the harbor. They were flying flags from all over the world. They were all empty.

Kip got the feeling he was entering a very strange new world.

Welcome to the Wild West

One day in September 1848 an African American miner was walking along the San Francisco water-front. He heard someone calling to him—it was a wealthy white traveler who wanted some-one to carry his bags. This guy may have been used to bossing around slaves back east. But things were different out west. The black man pulled a bag from his pocket, showed off more than one hundred dollars in gold, and said: "Do you think I'll lug trunks when I can get that much in one day?"

"What a Puzzling Place!"

"**T**his is the best place for black folks on the globe," one black miner wrote to his wife in Missouri. "All a man has to do is to work, and he will make money." This was enough to draw African Americans to California from all over the United States. Some were escaping from slavery; some were free men hoping to find enough gold to buy the freedom of family members still enslaved in the South.

"What a puzzling place it was!" Leonard Kip said soon after stepping ashore. "A continual stream of active population was winding among the casks and barrels, which blocked up the place where the sidewalks ought to have been."

Kip was amazed by the diversity of the crowds: white and black Americans, Chinese, Mexicans, Germans, Chileans, Irish, Native Americans, Hawaiians—all with different styles of hair and dress, speaking different languages, racing between stores, bars, music halls, and gambling houses. "The town seems running wild after amusement," he said.

And wild after money too. By the time travelers got to San Francisco they were so feverish to find gold that some started digging for it right in the streets of town. And they often found it! What they didn't know was that the streets had been "salted," or secretly

sprinkled with gold dust. This was done by creative store owners who wanted to get people excited, then sell them mining gear at shockingly high prices.

Another clever merchant heard complaints about the enormous rats that were eating (and pooping on) all the food in the city. He imported a ship full of cats from Mexico. They sold out quickly (at eight to twelve dollars each).

Then there was the guy who declared he was a doctor and started seeing patients. No one in town was aware that he had no medical training at all—until someone he knew from back east showed up and demanded: "What do you know about being a doctor?"

"Well, not much," the man admitted. In his own defense he added: "I kill just as few as any of them."

Luckily for this guy, people were too busy making money to worry about small details. One such detail: the city's dirt streets got so muddy that crates, dogs, horses, and sometimes people, actually sank under the surface and rotted beneath the stinky brown ooze. (A sign on one street warned travelers that the way was not safe for man or beast: "This street is impassable, not even jackassable.")

People were too busy to worry that no one nearby was growing food, and that everything had to be shipped in from thousands of miles away. The result was incredibly high prices. "Money here goes like dirt; everything costs a dollar or dollars," said an astonished twenty-one-year-old named Enos Christman. Back home he could have bought a big bag of potatoes for a few pennies. "Today I purchased a single potato for forty-five cents."

But what did any of this matter when there was gold to be found? Most people stayed in town only long enough to buy supplies. Then they headed east for what they called "the diggings"—the gold-rich streams flowing down from the Sierra Nevada.

Off to the Diggings

As soon as he arrived at the diggings, a hopeful miner from Britain named William Ryan ran into an old friend.

"Good morning, Firmore," Ryan said to his friend.

"What, you!" Firmore shouted, shaking Ryan's hand. "How did you come, and where did you start from? You are looking all the worse for wear."

Ryan looked over his friend—at his shredded clothes, his filthy whiskers, his face caked with dirt. "I can't say you look quite as dapper, Firmore, as you did the day we went ashore."

Firmore confessed that he had been having tough times. "For several days after I got here, I did not make anything," he explained. "But since then I have, by the hardest work, averaged about seven dollars a day."

William Ryan

This surprised Ryan. Like most new miners, he knew nothing about gold mining. But he imagined it was pretty easy. You just bend down and collect the shiny nuggets, right?

"Ah! It's more luck than anything," Firmore said. "But, luck or no luck, no man can pick up gold, even here, without the very hardest labor, and that's a fact. Some think that it is only to come here, squat down anywhere, and pick away. But they soon find out their mistake. I never knew what hard work was until I came here."

When you read letters and journals of miners in California, you see lots of stories like Firmore's. People came with dreams of scooping up glittering lumps of gold. And this did happen once in a while (one miner found a hunk of solid gold weighing 195 pounds). But most miners spent long days squatting in chilly streams, scooping up pans full of dirt. After filling the pan with water, the miner gently rocked the pan back and forth, allowing the water to carry off the dirt little by little. Flakes and dust-size bits of gold (if there were any) collected at the bottom of the pan, because gold is about eight times heavier than dirt.

"There is gold here in abundance," one miner said of the California diggings. "But it requires patience and hard labor, with some skill and experience to obtain it."

Or, as another disappointed miner put it: "The chances of making a fortune in the gold mines are about the same as those in favor of drawing a prize in a lottery."

There was still good money to be made, though. Miners who were lucky enough to find a good spot, and who worked from sunup to sundown, were often able to collect one to two ounces of gold a day. An ounce of gold was worth sixteen dollars. Back east, in comparison, skilled workers earned about $1.50 for a twelve-hour day.

So you can see why people kept coming to California. As one miner explained to his wife: "I am willing to stand it all to make enough to get us a home, and so I can be independent of some of the darned [censored] that felt themselves above me because I was poor."

Gettin' Crowded Out Here

Nearly 100,000 people raced to California in 1849. They even earned their own nickname: "forty-niners." Thousands more were on the way. In fact, this was the largest movement of people the world had ever seen. Gold can do that.

One result: the most promising gold mining spots were getting crowded with tents, shacks, and miners. And garbage. One miner described walking along a stream "strewn with old boots, hats, shirts, old sardine boxes, empty tins of preserved oysters, empty bottles, worn-out pots and kettles."

Desperate miners were digging in the streams, along the banks, even in the streets of the mining camp. One woman found gold flakes while sweeping the dirt floor of her shack. She shoved aside the table, started digging, and found hundreds of dollars' worth of gold.

Most miners' experience was more like that of William Swain, who had come west from his farm in New York. "My first day's work in the business was an ounce," he wrote to his wife. "The second was $35, and third was $92." That was followed by day after day when he found nothing. Meanwhile, the high price of food and supplies was eating away at his little pile of gold. Swain had boldly promised to bring home $10,000. "As soon as I can get the rocks in my pocket I shall hasten home as fast as steam can carry me," he told his family.

"O! William, I cannot wait much longer," his wife, Sabrina, wrote to him. "I want to see you so bad."

"I must have the $10,000," Swain insisted.

But in a letter to his brother, Swain admitted that things were going badly. "George, I tell you, mining among the mountains is a dog's life," he said. He even warned George to give up any dreams of gold mining. "There was some talk between us of your coming to this country," Swain wrote. "For God's sake think not of it. Stay at home."

Still, Swain was committed to staying long enough to make his fortune. So were thousands of others. Just how eager were these miners to find some gold? One day at a mining camp, a miner died and his friends gathered for the funeral. They knelt around an open grave as a fellow miner (and former minister) started reading some prayers.

After a few minutes, the minds of the grieving miners started drifting toward dreams of gold. Their hands started sifting through the dirt that had been dug up from the grave.

The minister saw that the men weren't paying attention to the service. He opened his mouth to complain, but then he noticed what they had noticed— yellow flecks in the dirt.

"Boys, what's that?" he asked. He took a closer look, then answered his own question:

"Gold! And the richest kind o' diggings!

The congregation are dismissed!"

R.I.P.
1515
-1849

The dead man was dragged away to be buried somewhere else, while the minister ran off for his mining shovel and pan.

I've Got a Better Idea

Wasn't there an easier way to make money than sifting through dirt from your dead friend's grave? Definitely.

The surest way to make money in California was not to *be* a gold miner but to *sell stuff* to gold miners. Merchants made fortunes selling food, mining supplies, and clothes—gladly taking miners' gold in exchange. In mining camp bars, the price for a glass of whiskey was one pinch of gold dust (which explains why bar owners liked to hire bartenders with fat fingers).

When a twenty-four-year-old Jewish immigrant named Levi Strauss arrived in San Francisco, he was amazed to see store owners racing each other out to his ship in rowboats, each shouting that he would buy all the goods on board. The local stores must be pretty busy, Strauss figured. He set up his own shop, where miners told him they were always looking for pants that wouldn't fall apart on them. So Strauss and a friend invented a new kind of pants, made from tough denim fabric, dyed blue, and held together with metal rivets. And that's how blue jeans were born.

Women in California saw other moneymaking opportunities—ones the men had missed. There were no laundries in San Francisco, for example. Most men just walked around in smelly shirts. Those who were picky about cleanliness sent their clothes to be washed in Hawaii or China, then waited six months to get them back. Women started local laundries (and offered much quicker service).

When Luzena Stanley Wilson came to California with her husband and kids in 1849, she had the usual dreams of finding a fortune in gold. But soon she discovered a much better way to make money. She was bending over a campfire, cooking dinner for her family, when a hungry miner walked up and said: "I'll give you five dollars, ma'am, for them biscuits."

"It sounded like a fortune to me," she said. She stood there silently, too surprised to answer.

The man thought she was driving a hard bargain. He took out a ten-dollar gold piece and dropped it into her hand.

"I made some more biscuits for my family," she remembered.

The next day, as the family drove into Sacramento, the coin fell from a box and rolled out though the bottom of the wagon. But Wilson knew where to get more.

Sure enough, as she cooked at her family's campsite a few days later, a man walked up and got right to business:

Luzena Stanley Wilson

"Madame, I want a good substantial breakfast, cooked by a woman."

"I asked him what he would have," Wilson said.

"Two onions, two eggs, a beef-steak, and a cup of coffee."

"He ate it, thanked me, and gave me five dollars," she said. "If I had asked ten dollars he would have paid it."

The family sold their oxen and put the money into a restaurant and hotel. The profits were piling up—until they lost everything in a flood. So they moved on to another mining town, where Wilson started selling meals again. She soon saved enough to buy a new hotel and was making great money—until they lost everything in a fire.

"I, as before, set up my stove and camp kettle," Wilson said. She started all over again, selling meals to miners, and saving up to buy a bigger business . . .

Well, no one said life out west was going to be easy.

Advancing Civilization?

One day a miner named Daniel Knower walked into a store and paid for his supplies with gold dust, as miners always did. The store owner weighed the dust and told Knower what it was worth. But the figure seemed too low. Knower asked the man to weigh the gold again.

"He came back in a few minutes and apologized," Knower remembered, "saying that he had weighed it in the scales that he used when he traded with the Indians."

Many mining town merchants were doing the same thing. They had two scales to weigh gold: one for whites and one for Native Americans (gold always seemed to weigh less on the scale used for Native Americans).

This brings up an important point about the gold rush: it looked very different from different points of view. Even though most American miners never struck it rich, they saw the search as the adventure of a lifetime. "It is far more pleasing to me than to sit daily locked up in a dirty office," said one miner from Pennsylvania.

To the Indians of California, the gold rush looked less like an adventure and more like an invasion. Miners drove away the deer and other game that Indians had always relied on for food. They chopped down forests and polluted salmon streams. When some Native Americans tried to join the search for gold, they were violently driven away from good mining spots. And as had happened in Oregon, newcomers brought new diseases that devastated the native villages.

Everyone saw this happening, but to many Americans it seemed like a necessary step toward making California part of the United States. The *San Francisco Bulletin* put it bluntly: "It is a painful necessity of advancing civilization that the Indians should gradually disappear."

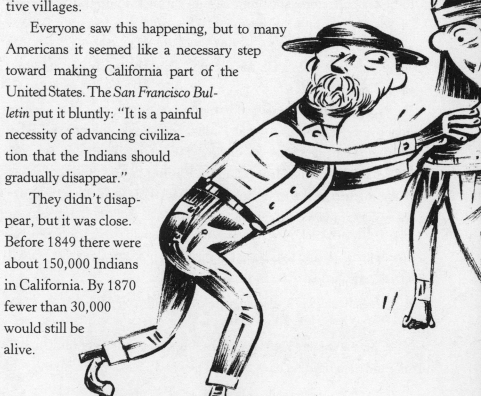

They didn't disappear, but it was close. Before 1849 there were about 150,000 Indians in California. By 1870 fewer than 30,000 would still be alive.

"California for the Americans!"

Meanwhile, miners from Mexico, Chile, China, France, and other countries were having their own troubles.

As more and more people crowded into the mining camps, some American miners turned angrily against those they saw as unwelcome competition for the scarce gold. "California for the Americans!" shouted American miners (perhaps forgetting that California had been part of the United States for only a year).

California's government responded in 1850 with the Foreign Miners' Tax, requiring foreign-born miners to pay a fee every month to stay at the mines. Tax collectors (and people pretending to be tax collectors) starting roaming through immigrants' mining camps, demanding the payment. This often led to fights. "I was sorry to stab the poor creature," one collector said after viciously snatching cash from a Chinese miner. "But the law makes it necessary to collect the tax."

None of this stopped the flow of foreign miners to California. Facing poverty, famine, and war in China, young men excitedly talked of California as *Gum Shan,* or Golden Mountain. By 1852 more than 20,000 men had sailed from China to California, and thousands more made the trip in the following years. Back home in China, wives of the absent miners were singing a new song:

> *Oh, don't ever marry your daughter to a man from Gold*
> *   Mountain.*
> *Lonely and sad—a cooking pot is her only companion.*

Chinese miners dreamed of finding some quick gold in California, and then heading back home. They had a hard time with the gold part. The tax on foreign miners was one problem. Another was that American miners kept chasing them off any decent mining site they happened to find. Most of them stayed on in California, though, determined to find new opportunities.

Remember these guys. They're going to play a major role in the story of the West.

The Mystery of Joaquin Murrieta

Mexican miners were clashing with Americans as well. There was plenty of leftover anger from the recent U.S.-Mexican War. Also, many Mexicans had mining experience and were good at digging gold, which some Americans found annoying.

This hostility led to one of the most famous stories of the gold rush. According to one version, it all began one day when a young miner from Mexico named Joaquin Murrieta was riding a horse that belonged to his brother. A group of American miners thought they recognized the horse as one that had been stolen from them, and they approached Murrieta. One of the Americans said:

"You are the chap that's been a'stealing horses and mules around here, for the last six months, are you?"

"You charge me unjustly," replied Murrieta. "I borrowed this horse of my half brother, who bought it from an American, which he can easily prove."

"You are nothing but a dirty thief!" the American yelled.

"Hang him! Hang him!" the others shouted.

The men pulled Murrieta off the horse, tied him up, and dragged him to his brother's cabin. They wrapped a rope around his brother's neck and hanged him from a tree. Then they tied Murrieta to the same tree and whipped him while his brother's body swung back and forth from the branch above.

After burying his brother's body that night, Murrieta swore he would never rest until he spilled the blood of his enemies. One by one, over the following weeks, the men who had attacked him were found dead at their campsites. And from that point on, no American miner was safe from Murrieta's fury.

At least, this is how the story went in a book called *The Life and Adventures of Joaquin Murrieta, the Celebrated California Bandit*, published in 1854 by a Cherokee Indian author named Yellow Bird. Yellow Bird claimed to have collected the tale from local sources. He must have made up the dialogue, though, and probably some of the details too.

But he definitely didn't make up the person. There really was a miner named Joaquin Murrieta who moved with his family from Mexico to the California mines in 1850. Murrieta family members report that Joaquin and his brother were attacked just as the book described.

Murrieta shows up in California newspapers too, which printed story after story about "the notorious outlaw, Joaquin." The papers described Murrieta as a vicious killer who led a band of bloody thieves, including a three-fingered sidekick named Manuel "Tres Dedos" Garcia. But to Mexicans he became a heroic figure, a Robin Hood battling back against gold-grabbing Americans.

Soon after the governor of California offered a five-thousand-dollar reward for capture of Joaquin Murrieta, a company of rangers surrounded what they believed to be his gang. They shot the men, cut off Joaquin's head, put it in a jar of brandy, brought it back to town, and charged people a dollar to see it. They didn't seem to mind that people who knew Murrieta said it was not his head.

For years after this, people continued to claim they had seen the mysterious Joaquin—or to have been robbed by him. What really happened to Joaquin Murrieta? No one knows.

Time to Give Up?

Now back to the diggings, where it was getting harder and harder for miners to make a living. Most of the easy-to-find gold had already been found.

"I have no pile yet," one miner wrote home. "But you can bet your life I will never come home until I have something more than when I started."

Most of the miners felt that way—it was embarrassing to go home empty-handed. But the longer they stayed, the more homesick they got. "I feel bad sometimes when I think of home," James Maxfeld wrote to his wife in Massachusetts. "Then again, come to think of how dull it is at home, I do not want to be there."

Four months later Maxfeld was a changed man. "I want to be home," he wrote. "I would give anything I have got for the privilege of having a kiss from you."

Another miner expressed his loneliness in his diary: "Got nearer to a female this evening than I have been for six months. Came near fainting."

No wives or girlfriends, very little gold to be found, ridiculously expensive food and supplies, backs aching from working bent over, legs swelling from standing in freezing streams . . . all this was enough to cure most miners of gold fever. Miners expressed their disappointment in new songs like "The Lousy Miner," which was often heard in 1850s California:

It's four long years since I reached this land,
In search among the rocks and sand;
And yet I'm poor when the truth is told,
I'm a lousy miner,
I'm a lousy miner in search of shining gold.

There was still plenty of gold out there, but it was stuck in the rocks deep underground and getting it required expensive equipment. By the mid-1850s big companies were taking over the gold mining business from individual miners.

William Swain was one of thousands of miners who decided it was time to give up. "I have made up my mind that I have got enough of California and am coming home as fast as I can," he wrote. Gone were his dreams of marching back to his family with a fortune. "I shall get home with only $700 or $800," he warned his wife. "But I am thankful for small favors."

Historians estimate that of all the people who came to California in search of gold, only one in twenty left the diggings richer than when he arrived. Swain was just happy to get home, especially when he saw that the entire town had come out to greet him. "I have been many miles and seen many places," he said, "but this is the finest sight I have ever seen."

Maybe I'll Stay

Others decided to settle in California. This was easier said than done, for some.

Biddy Mason and her three young daughters wanted to stay. Unfortunately for them, Robert Smith was determined to leave. Smith held the Mason family as slaves—even though California had joined the Union as a free state in 1850.

By 1855 Smith realized that Biddy Mason knew slavery was illegal in California. That's when he announced it was time to move to Texas (where slavery was legal). Mason had no intention of going. She contacted free black friends in Los Angeles and told them her story. The friends went to a local judge, who agreed to hear her case.

In a courthouse packed with curious spectators, Robert Smith tried to claim that Mason and her daughters weren't really slaves. He treated them just like family, he insisted.

Mason saw things differently, as she told the judge:

"I always feared this trip to Texas, since I first heard of it. Mr. Smith told me I would be just as free in Texas as here."

She didn't believe that. Neither did the judge, who ruled that Mason and her daughters were free and could live wherever they wanted. They joined the growing black community in Los Angeles.

Biddy Mason

But Wait, There's More!

Biddy Mason was one of thousands who chose to stay and build a future in California. By 1860 the state population would zoom toward 400,000.

California's quick growth was one major effect of the gold rush. Another effect: many of the miners who caught gold fever were never really cured. As they headed back home, they couldn't help themselves—they kept looking for gold.

That's what George Jackson was doing in the Rocky Mountains in January 1859. It was much too late in winter to be out in these snowy mountains, but Jackson had heard rumors of gold being spotted in the area. He decided to search for one more day before heading back to Denver (which then had a total of twenty buildings).

He found a promising-looking spot along Clear Creek. The dirt was frozen so solid, he had to build a fire on top of it before he could scoop some into his drinking cup. He swirled the cup around, slowly splashing out the dirt and water. Soon all that remained in the bottom of his cup was about an ounce of gold flakes.

"I went to bed and dreamed of riches galore," Jackson said. "I had struck it rich! There were millions in it!" News of Jackson's find set off a whole new gold rush, as more than 100,000 people raced to the Rocky Mountains of Colorado. And Jackson was right, there were millions of dollars of gold in those hills. Actually, there were hundreds of millions (though Jackson sold his mine for just a few thousand).

From Colorado, hopeful miners fanned out all over the West. It was "a mad, furious race for wealth," one miner said. In June 1859 the furious race led a miner named Henry "Old Pancake" Comstock to a rocky hillside in the desert of western Nevada.

Comstock got his nickname because he was too lazy to bake bread and always used his flour to fry piles of pancakes. But Old Pancake was feeling energetic on this day. It paid off—he stumbled onto one of the biggest mineral strikes in world history. Or, more precisely, he stumbled onto two Irish immigrants who had already found the spot. Comstock liked the looks of it, so he started shouting that the land was his. He was so loud and annoying that the Irish guys finally agreed to make him a partner.

The men spent a few weeks digging, finding several ounces of gold a day. They could have gotten even more if it weren't for the heavy bluish sand that kept caking to their boots and shovels. They were constantly stopping to scrape the stuff off and toss it aside.

Finally someone decided to bring a bit of this irritating sand to a nearby town to find out what it was. The answer: nearly pure silver. This sparked yet another rush, this time to the desert of Nevada. Miners founded the booming town of Virginia City. And Old Pancake's mine, which became known as the Comstock Lode, produced four hundred million dollars in silver and gold over the next thirty years.

The Ten-Day Millionaire

One of the thousands racing to Nevada was a young man from Missouri named Samuel Clemens.

Clemens traveled by stagecoach, which was by far the fastest way to cross the West. By stopping often at stations to trade tired horses for fresh ones, stagecoaches could get you from St. Louis to San Francisco in just twenty-five days (compared to the four months it took people who traveled in their own wagons).

Clemens did point out some drawbacks, however. Passengers were quickly coated with dust and bugs. And Clemens and the other passengers sat facing each other on benches, packed so tightly that knees bumped. This was only a little painful on smooth sections of road. But when they hit holes and rocks (which were everywhere), passengers smashed together and sent each other flying.

"First we would all

be down in a pile at the

forward end of the stage, nearly in

a sitting posture, and in a second we would

shoot to the other end, and stand on our

heads."

Samuel Clemens

Bags of mail, luggage, loose books, pipes, canteens, even pistols, went flying around the car. People shouted:

"Can't you quit crowding?"

"Take your elbow out of my ribs!"

This continued day and night for more than three weeks. Passengers could get out for only about twenty minutes at a time, when the coach stopped at a station to change animals.

Clemens survived the journey and immediately started searching for silver and gold. And as he later wrote in his book *Roughing It* (full of great stories and great exaggerations) he and two friends really did find a rich mine. So rich, in fact, that one of the partners was offered $200,000 (about $3 million in today's money) for his share—and he refused it!

Much too excited to sleep, Clemens and his partner Calvin Higbie spent the night dreaming of how to spend their fortunes.

Clemens: *Cal, what kind of house are you going to build?*

Higbie: *I was thinking about that. Three-story and an attic.*

Clemens: *But what kind?*

Higbie: *Well, I don't hardly know. Brick, I suppose.*

Clemens: *Brick—bosh.*

Higbie: *Why? What is your idea?*

Clemens: *Brownstone front—French plate glass—billiard room off the dining room—statuary and paintings . . .*

Higbie: *By George!*

According to the law, the finder of a mine had ten days to start working at the site. If he didn't do any work in that time, he lost his claim. Higbie had to help on another job for a few days, but he left a note for Clemens: "Don't fail to do the work before the ten days expire."

Clemens never saw the note. The next morning he heard a friend was very sick and hurried off to help. He left a note for Higbie, telling Higbie to start the work without him.

The third partner, meanwhile, thought the other two were starting the work.

When Clemens got back to their cabin ten days later, he saw Higbie inside, slumped in a chair, looking stunned.

"Higbie, what—what is it?"

"We're ruined," Higbie said. "We didn't do the work."

The ten days had passed. The land was now open to the public again. Other miners were already digging there.

"I was absolutely and unquestionably worth a million dollars, once, for ten days," Clemens later said.

What Next?

"**W**hat to do next?" Clemens wondered. Like so many failed miners, he was ashamed to go back home with nothing to show for his efforts. He thought about the jobs he had done since he was thirteen.

"I had once been a grocery clerk, for one day," he remembered, "but had consumed so much sugar in that time that I was relieved from further duty."

He had worked in a bookstore, but didn't like it. Customers kept bothering him while he was trying to read. He had been a blacksmith, law student, drugstore clerk, printer, riverboat pilot . . .

The one thing he actually enjoyed was writing funny stories. Since coming west he had sent some stories to Nevada newspapers. Much to his shock, they printed them. Just as Clemens was thinking this over, he got a letter from a Virginia City paper offering him work as a reporter. He took the job. Just for fun, he started signing his articles with the name Mark Twain.

This kind of thing was happening a lot—people kept coming west to search for gold, failing, and deciding to stay anyway. They found new jobs, started new businesses, built new towns.

That didn't mean life was easy in the West. One of westerners' main complaints was that they felt cut off from the rest of the United States. It took months for mail and news to travel from the East to the West. Whenever a ship with mail finally arrived in San Francisco, thousands rushed to the post office—often with blankets under their arms. They knew they could be waiting outside for days while post office clerks sorted through the mail. Merchants came along selling coffee and sandwiches. Others earned extra cash by waiting in line until they got close to the post office entrance, then selling their spot to the highest bidder.

Things were getting ridiculous. There had to be a faster way to get letters and news across the country. Someone in the government had the idea of importing camels from Saudi Arabia, loading them with mail sacks, and leading them across the deserts of the West. The camels were not pleased. First the rocky roads ripped up their hooves. Then mail carriers tried tying leather boots on the camels' feet.

Soon after this unfortunate experiment, a group of stagecoach owners introduced a better mail delivery service. They called it Russell, Majors & Waddell's Central Overland California & Pike's Peak Express Company.

Luckily for them, customers came up with a catchier name: the Pony Express.

Out of the Way
of the Big Engine

"I was just eighteen, and boy-like, craved such ex-citement," remembered a Pony Express rider named William Campbell. But as Campbell quickly realized, galloping across the West was, as he put it, "more hard work than fun." During one run Campbell nearly crashed into a pack of bloody-faced wolves that were ripping flesh from some big dead thing. "They refused to move when I rode at them," he said, "and my horse shied at the smell of blood and animals." Campbell swerved around the wolves and raced on.

The Rise and Fall of the Pony Express

The Pony Express started doing business in April 1860. For five dollars a letter, you could have Express riders carry your mail from Missouri (where the eastern railroads ended) 1,950 miles to California in just ten days—by far the fastest mail service available at the time.

The whole thing worked like a giant relay race. Each rider was assigned a section of the route, usually about eighty miles. The rider's job was to speed across his section, stopping at stations every ten or fifteen miles to change horses. At the end of his route, the rider handed the mailbags to the next guy. Then he could collapse onto a cot for a few hours before jumping up, grabbing new mail sacks, and racing back the other way.

The company liked to hire young men, tough teenagers who had grown up riding horses. When Elijah Wilson took the job, he was told the most important rule: "When we started out we were not to turn back, no matter what happened." This made life dangerous for riders, especially as they crossed Native American territory. Indians didn't welcome riders cutting through their hunting grounds, using their scarce water resources.

One day Wilson was stopped by an Indian warrior and given a warning. "He said I had no right to cross their country," Wilson remembered. "The land belonged to the Indians, and they were going to drive the white men out of it." But turning around was not an option.

While resting at a station in Nevada a while later, Wilson and a few other riders were attacked. "One of the Indians shot me in the head with a flint-tipped arrow," he said. His friends tried to pull out the arrow, but the pointed stone stuck fast in his skull. "Thinking that

I would surely die, they rolled me under a tree and started for the next station as fast as they could go. "They got a few men and came back the next morning to bury me; but when they got to me and found that I was still alive, they thought they would not bury me just then."

Wilson lay unconscious for the next eighteen days. "Then I began to get better fast," he remembered. "It was not long before I was riding again."

The Pony Express failed—but obviously not because the riders weren't tough enough. The real problem was, it was just too expensive to maintain all those stations, horses, and riders. The company lost money steadily. Then, in October 1861, American engineers finished building the first transcontinental telegraph—a telegraph line all the way across the country. Suddenly short messages could be sent over wires from east to west. That put the Pony Express out of business once and for all.

The telegraph was the perfect technology for quick communication. But was there any way to move people and goods across the country more quickly? Yes: build a transcontinental railroad.

The only problem? No one had ever built a railroad that long. Most Americans were pretty sure it was impossible.

Here Comes Crazy Judah

Theodore Judah disagreed.

Growing up in New York, Judah had enrolled in college engineering classes when he was eleven. He began designing railroads when he was still a teenager. By 1861 Judah was in California, thinking about building a transcontinental railroad. "It will be built," he said over and over, "and I am going to have something to do with it."

Judah's wife, Anna, said that her husband talked so much about the railroad, he was beginning to annoy the entire city of Sacramento. He would corner people on the street and start describing his plans.

Anna would nudge him and whisper, "Theodore, those people don't care."

"But we must keep the ball rolling," he would insist.

And Californians really did want a railroad to connect them to the rest of the country. They just didn't think it could be done. For starters, how could anyone build tracks up and over the sharp slopes of the Sierra Nevada mountain range? Judah kept insisting he could do it. That's when people started calling him "Crazy Judah."

Never one to be easily discouraged, Judah made more than twenty trips into the Sierra Nevada, carefully mapping out the route a railroad could take. Anna often came along to make drawings and paintings of the route. All this work finally began to pay off when a group of local business owners agreed to invest some money to start building the railroad east out of Sacramento.

Theodore rushed to his wife with the news:

"Anna, if you want to see the first work done on the Pacific

railroad, look out your bedroom window. I am going to work there

this morning and I am going to have these men pay for it!"

Theodore Judah

Anna Judah

"It's about time that someone else helped!" Anna said.

It was a good start, but Judah knew that a project this massive would require thousands of workers and millions of dollars. So he packed up his maps and Anna's paintings and sailed to Washington to persuade government leaders to support the transcontinental railroad. Judah showed up in the capital in October 1861—just as the Civil War was ripping the United States in two. In a weird way, his timing was pretty good.

The Race for Miles—and Money

The new president of the United States was Abraham Lincoln (turns out his opposition to the U.S.-Mexican War didn't end his career in politics after all). Lincoln was all for the transcontinental railroad, saying it was "demanded in the interests of the whole country." Or, what was left of the whole country. Eleven states had just dropped out of the Union. Lincoln was desperate not to lose any more—especially not California (and its gold). His hope was that a rail line from the East to the West would help bind California to the rest of the United States.

In the Pacific Railroad Act of 1862, Congress declared that two companies would basically race to build the transcontinental railroad. Theodore Judah and his Central Pacific Railroad would start in Sacramento and build east. At the same time, the Union Pacific Railroad would build west from Nebraska, where the current westbound rail lines ended. The government would pay each company for every mile of track completed. Both companies could continue building, and collecting money, until they ran into each other—wherever that happened to be.

The race was on.

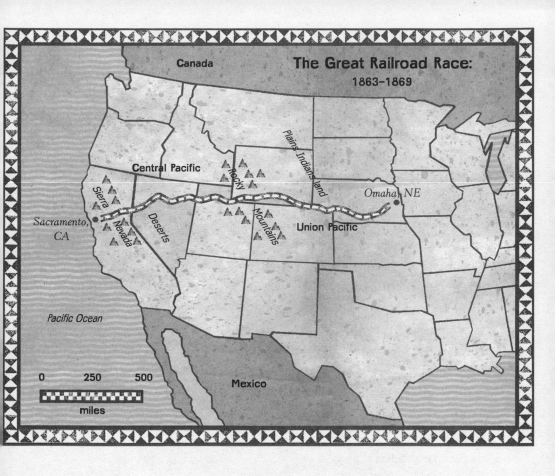

The Great Railroad Race:
1863–1869

Canada

Central Pacific

Rocky Mountains

Plains Indians land

Omaha, NE

Union Pacific

Sierra Nevada

Deserts

Sacramento, CA

Pacific Ocean

0   250   500
miles

Mexico

How to Steal Millions: Part I

"**T**his is the grandest enterprise under God!" declared one Union Pacific investor when the work began in Omaha, Nebraska, in 1863. Turns out it was also a grand opportunity to rip off the American taxpayer. The Union Pacific vice president Thomas Durant was honest about this (in private, that is). He outlined his plan:

"Grab a wad of money from the construction fees—

and get out."

Thomas Durant

Durant's scheme was pretty confusing, but here's the basic idea. He set up a construction company, keeping it secret that he actually controlled it. Then he had the Union Pacific hire his construction company to build the railroad. His company started ed building on the flat land along the Platte River. Construction cost about $30,000 a mile. But he had his company claim that the work was costing $50,000 a mile. The Union Pacific collected money from investors and the government, then used that money to pay Durant's construction company $50,000 per mile. Durant's company pocketed the extra $20,000. (Members of Congress didn't complain, possibly because Durant had quietly handed many of them stock in his company.)

The UP's chief engineer, Peter Dey, sensed that something suspicious was happening. "No man can call $50,000 per mile for a road up the Platte Valley anything else but a big swindle," he said.

How to Steal Millions: Part II

Dey was even more upset when Durant starting messing with the route of the railroad. Dey designed a road that went out of Omaha and headed straight west for fourteen miles. To Durant, this was a wasted opportunity. The government was paying for every mile of track, right? So Durant brought in a different engineer to design a new route—one with a big, totally unnecessary curve that added nine miles to the route.

"This part of the road was located with great care by me," Dey objected.

Durant ignored the objection. Dey quit in protest. The work went on without him.

How to Steal Millions: Part III

In California the four directors of the Central Pacific, known as the "Big Four," were working some schemes of their own. The Pacific Railroad Act declared that the government would pay the railroad companies extra for each mile of track built through mountains. This was fair, since it was more difficult and expensive to construct railroads through mountains. It gave the Big Four an idea.

The Sierra Nevada slopes began rising about twenty miles east of Sacramento. But the Big Four hired an expert geologist to declare that the mountains actually started just seven miles east of town. To nonexperts the land looked flat. But the expert insisted it was really a mountain. The Big Four sent the geologist's report to Washington, charging the government the higher rate to build tracks over this "mountainous" land. And the Central Pacific collected an extra $500,000 in government payments.

"There is cheating on the grandest scale in all these railroads," declared the *New York Herald*. Theodore Judah agreed. And as the railroad's chief engineer, he refused to accept such bogus profits. He charged into the offices of the Big Four, and some serious shouting matches followed. Angry and frustrated, Judah sailed from California to New York in October 1863. His hope: to find new investors to buy the Central Pacific. He started feeling feverish while crossing Panama, and by the time he reached New York City he was flat on his back and barely conscious. His wife, Anna, had him carried ashore and put in a carriage. "I kept him up by dipping my finger in the brandy bottle and having him take it that way," she said.

That was about all Anna could do for her husband. He died of yellow fever a week later, at age thirty-seven, and was buried beneath a tombstone that read, "He rests from his labors."

Who's Going to Build This Thing?

Judah may have rested, but the race he had started was just beginning. For a race, it was off to a pretty slow start.

When work began in Sacramento, people gathered to cheer and wave signs that said things like "Little Indian Boy, Step Out of the Way of the Big Engine." This cruel motto captured the mood. Americans sensed that this railroad was going to change the country forever. Assuming it could actually be built, that is. There were no factories in California yet. So the Central Pacific had to get nearly all of its supplies shipped from the East: locomotives, train cars, iron rails, even the nails.

Collis Huntington had the job of buying supplies in New York City and shipping them to his partners in California. One of the Big Four, Huntington really *was* big: over six feet tall and 250 pounds. (His son, he bragged, was even bigger: "My son weighs 275 pounds; my son is sixteen.")

His attitude was big too. It had to be. He often bought supplies for the railroad with no idea how he was going to pay for them. "I have gone to sleep at night in New York," he said, "when I had a million and a half dollars to be paid by three o'clock on the following day, without knowing where the money was coming from—and slept soundly."

That's the attitude you need to take on a project this huge. You also need people to do the actual work. That was becoming a problem. When the Central Pacific advertised for five thousand workers, only eight hundred showed up. After a couple weeks of swinging picks and shovels, many of the men collected their pay and quit to try for easier earnings in the gold mines.

Meanwhile, across the West in Nebraska, the Union Pacific was moving only a tiny bit faster—laying just twenty miles of track by

1864. Like Central Pacific, the UP had a hard time finding workers. (A little something called the Civil War was going on back east. That kept a few million American men busy.)

The UP was about to face another problem, as a young engineer named James Evans realized while planning the railroad's route through western Nebraska. Evans watched a group of Lakota warriors ride up to his crew. The chief got right to the point:

"I do not like the idea of

your coming here. This is the

Indian's country."

That pretty much sums up the trouble—the planned route of the Union Pacific sliced through hundreds of miles of Plains Indians' land. These nations had horses and guns, and thousands of young men who knew how to use them. No wonder government leaders worried about what they called the "Indian Problem."

An Old Problem Gets Worse

This was not a new problem. Since the days of the Oregon Trail, settlers, miners, and stagecoaches had been cutting across Plains Indians' land. These travelers brought new diseases and shot buffalo, which the Indians depended on for food. Violent clashes between settlers and Indians became more and more common.

And now, just as the railroad workers were arriving, the fighting exploded to a whole new level. In the summer of 1864, a group of Indian warriors killed a family of four in Colorado. Furious settlers brought the bodies into Denver and put them on display. "Everybody saw them," said one Denver resident, "and anger and revenge mounted all day long as the people filed past."

"I determined to strike a blow against this savage and determined foe," declared John Chivington, an American army officer.

Just before sunrise on November 29, Chivington led seven hundred soldiers toward a Cheyenne camp on the banks of Sand Creek. In the camp were about six hundred Indians, most of them women and children.

"Kill and scalp all, big and little," Colonel Chivington told his men.

A young officer objected. "It would be murder in every sense of the word," he said, arguing that the people in this camp had nothing to do with recent attacks on white settlers.

"I have come to kill Indians," Chivington insisted.

Sand Creek and Beyond

"I was still in bed when I heard shouts and the noise of people running about the camp," George Bent later reported.

The son of a Cheyenne mother and white father, Bent was living with the Cheyenne at Sand Creek when Chivington's soldiers attacked. He jumped up and scrambled out of his tent. "All was confusion and noise," he said. "Men, women, and children rushing out of the lodges partly dressed."

Hundreds of Americans soldiers were charging into camp from several directions. "Remember the murdered women and children!" Chivington shouted. "Take no prisoners!"

The Indian men dove back into their tents to get their guns and bows. A young Cheyenne named Little Bear said the bullets smacking his tent sounded "like big hailstones."

George Bent grabbed his rifle and ran out to join the fight. But the Cheyenne fighters were nearly surrounded by American soldiers and were slowly driven out of their camp. "I was struck in the hip by a bullet and knocked down," Bent said.

With the help of friends, Bent made it to another Cheyenne camp nearby. Other survivors from the Sand Creek battle also gathered there. "Everyone was crying," said Bent, "even the warriors, and the women and

children screaming and wailing. Nearly everyone present had lost some relatives or friends."

What exactly happened at Sand Creek? John Chivington reported that he had attacked a village that had nine hundred to one thousand Cheyenne warriors. He said it was a fierce battle between American and Cheyenne soldiers, and that "between five hundred and six hundred Indians were left dead upon the ground."

Other witnesses—both American and Cheyenne—said they saw about 160 Cheyenne dead, including about 100 women and children. An army officer named James Conner described the fight as more massacre than battle. He said he saw U.S. soldiers killing women and children, cutting off their scalps and slicing up their bodies "in the most horrible manner."

A committee in Congress investigated the incident and concluded that something horrible had happened at Sand Creek. "As to Colonel Chivington," the members of Congress reported, "our committee can hardly find fitting terms to describe his conduct. Wearing the uniform of the United States . . . he deliberately planned and executed a foul and dastardly massacre."

Chivington retired from the army and was never punished. For the rest of his life he denied having killed women and children. "I stand by Sand Creek," he maintained.

But the Cheyenne told their own story of what they called the Sand Creek Massacre. The news sped across the Great Plains. Arapaho and Lakota warriors banded together with the Cheyenne in calls for revenge. "This was an uncommon thing, to begin a war in the dead of winter," said George Bent, "but the Cheyennes were very mad and would not wait."

Working in small, fast-riding groups, Indian fighters attacked stagecoaches, yanked down telegraph wires, and burned ranches all over Colorado. Early in 1865 a thousand Plains warriors attacked the town of Julesburg, Colorado, burning every building to the ground.

Even this didn't prevent settlers from coming west. Not when there was gold to be found.

War Spreads North

In August 1865 a Lakota chief named Red Cloud was camped near the Powder River in Montana. Hunters raced into camp with startling news: American settlers were pouring onto Lakota land! Miners had found gold in Montana and were now carving a wagon road right through Lakota hunting grounds.

"The white men have crowded the Indians back year by year," Red Cloud protested. He had this warning for the American "Great Father" (president, that is):

"If the Great Father kept white men out of my country, then peace would last forever. The Great Spirit has raised me in this land and has raised you in another land. What I have said I mean. I mean to keep this land."

Red Cloud

Government leaders believed him. And they badly wanted to keep war from spreading all over the Great Plains. But they badly wanted gold too. So in June 1866 they invited Red Cloud to a meeting at Fort Laramie, in what is now Wyoming. The government offer was this: we pay you money and you let American miners use the road through your land.

Red Cloud and the other Lakota didn't have time to respond. While the chiefs were still talking the offer over, seven hundred American soldiers showed up with orders to guard the road through Lakota land! "The Great Father sends us presents and wants us to sell him the road," shouted a fuming Red Cloud. "But the white chief goes with soldiers to steal the road before the Indians say yes or no!"

The Lakota chiefs stormed out of the meeting. And the American soldiers quickly chopped down trees and hammered together log forts along the miners' road—the Bozeman Trail, as it came to be known. This ignited a conflict called Red Cloud's War, as bands of Lakota warriors attacked travelers and soldiers along the road.

The soldiers were supposed to be guarding the road. But they were so badly outnumbered, they spent most of their time shivering in their forts (and eating their horses as the food ran out).

At Fort Phil Kearny an American officer named William Fetterman got sick of sitting around. Fetterman didn't respect Indians as soldiers. He was sure he could end the whole war with one bold attack. "Give me eighty men," he boasted, "and I would ride through the whole Sioux nation."

On a freezing morning in December 1866, Fetterman got his chance.

The Shocking Fetterman Fight

"I was sixteen years old when this happened," remembered a Lakota fighter named Fire Thunder. The respected warrior Crazy Horse set up the strategy. He knew that the Americans in Fort Phil Kearny must be getting low on firewood. He hid Fire Thunder and more than a thousand other Lakota, Cheyenne, and Arapaho warriors behind a nearby hill. He told them what to do. Then he waited.

As expected, a group of soldiers came out of the fort to cut wood. Crazy Horse attacked the woodcutters with a small group of warriors. The soldiers blasted bugles—a signal for help. William Fetterman charged out of the fort with (coincidentally) eighty soldiers.

Crazy Horse retreated to the top of a hill, trying to tempt Fetterman into attacking him. He taunted Fetterman by calmly walking around on the hill while Fetterman's soldiers fired at him. He even got off his horse and casually adjusted the saddle.

Fetterman couldn't take it anymore. He led his men on a charge up the hill—and right into Crazy Horse's trap.

"When they came to the bottom of the hill, the fighting began all at once," Fire Thunder said. In less than thirty minutes of brutal combat, Fetterman and all his men were killed. About two hundred Indian fighters were killed or wounded as well.

Fire Thunder was stunned by the scene: dead men and horses lying everywhere, frozen pools of blood all over the mud and snow.

When they heard about the Fetterman Fight, Americans were stunned too. This was the biggest battle American soldiers had ever fought with Indians, and it was a disastrous defeat.

The government tried again to talk peace with the Lakota chiefs. Red Cloud's position remained firm: no peace until settlers and soldiers left Lakota land. "When we see the soldiers moving away and the forts abandoned, then I will come and talk," Red Cloud said.

And Now Comes the Railroad

So now, with fights raging all over the Plains, the Union Pacific was about to cut into Plains Indians' land. Well, at least the UP had solved its labor problem. When the Civil War ended in April 1865, thousands of army veterans headed west in search of work on the railroads. So did lots of Irish immigrants and former slaves.

With 10,000 workers, the UP started building more than a mile of track a day across the Great Plains. Crews of "iron men" laid down the seven-hundred-pound iron rails, then teams of "spikers" came up behind them to hammer in spikes holding the rails in place. Rolling along at the end of the track was a long supply train—really more like a town

on wheels. There were train cars with warehouses, blacksmith shops, butchers, and kitchens, and several with bunk beds. (A teenage worker named Erastus Lockwood said the bunks were covered with fleas, so he and his friends preferred to sleep on the roof of the train.)

By October 1866 the UP tracks reached nearly 250 miles west of Omaha. Thomas Durant decided this called for a big party, and he invited politicians and investors to come celebrate the progress. Bands and magicians entertained the guests, while chefs prepared a menu of western specialties (such as "buffalo tongue" and "braized bear in port wine"). Then everyone went to sleep in fancy tents with mattresses.

Durant's guests were having a great time—until the next morning. It was then, according to the UP engineer Silas Seymour, that the partygoers were "startled from their slumbers by the most unearthly whoops and yells of the Indians." People stuck their heads out of their tents and were terrified to see Indians running through camp, shouting and waving tomahawks.

They were relieved to realize that this was all part of the party. These were Pawnees, allies of the Americans. Durant had paid them to put on this little show. He wanted his guests to feel like they had experienced the real live Wild West.

The tourists went home happy, and the Union Pacific continued building across the Great Plains. But as the workers moved farther west, they started laying tracks into the territory of powerful Plains Indians nations such as the Lakota, the Cheyenne, and the Arapaho. These groups were in no mood to join a celebration for a railroad through their land.

This Time for Real

Already alarmed by white settlers, gold seekers, and wagon roads, the Plains Indians saw the advancing railroad as the biggest threat yet to their way of life. They watched hunters hired by the Union Pacific shoot thousands of buffalo to feed railroad workers. And they knew the railroad would bring more soldiers and settlers to the Plains.

In August 1867, near Plum Creek in Nebraska, a Cheyenne named Porcupine was riding with a group of warriors when they saw a train for the first time. "We looked at it from a high ridge," he remembered. "Far off it was very small, but it kept coming and growing larger all the time, puffing out smoke and steam."

After the train passed, the men rode down to the tracks to take a closer look. "We talked of our troubles," Porcupine said. "We were feeling angry and said among ourselves that we ought to do something."

The warriors yanked down the telegraph wire that ran along the train track. They used it to tie a few heavy pieces of wood across the tracks. Then they sat by the tracks and waited.

Soon after dark they heard a rumbling sound. It was getting louder.

"It's coming," Porcupine said.

Race You to Utah

What was wrong with the telegraph line along the Union Pacific track? William Thompson got the job of finding out. "About nine o'clock Tuesday night," he said, "myself and five others left Plum Creek station, and started up the track on a hand car, to find the place where the break in the telegraph was." The men saw that something was blocking the tracks, but too late—the handcar slammed into a pile of wood and flew off the tracks, tossing Thompson and the other men into the air.

Thompson's Tale

As William Thompson and the other repairmen hit the ground, Porcupine and his fellow warriors jumped up with their weapons.

"We fired two or three shots," Thompson said, "and then, as the Indians pressed on us, we ran away."

Thompson hadn't gotten far when he felt a bullet rip through his right arm. He kept running. A Cheyenne warrior chased him down and clubbed him with a rifle. "He then took out his knife," Thompson said, "stabbed me in the neck, and making a twirl round his fingers with my hair, he commenced sawing and hacking away at my scalp."

William Thompson was one of the few people to be scalped and live to tell about it. "I can't describe it to you," he later told a newspaper writer. "It just felt as if the whole head was taken right off."

Somehow Thompson managed to stay silent, convincing his attacker he was already dead. "The Indian then mounted and galloped away," Thompson said, "but as he went he dropped my scalp within a few feet of me."

Thompson grabbed back his scalp and hid in the weeds. He watched the Cheyenne warriors lay more wood across the tracks. He heard a train coming and wanted desperately to jump up to signal a warning, but he was too scared. The train was knocked off the tracks and skidded sideways onto the grass. The Cheyenne shot the men driving the train, then robbed and burned the train cars.

When the Indians rode away Thompson was finally able to get up and look for help. Two days later a reporter named Henry Stanley met him in Omaha. "In a pail of water by his side, was his scalp," Stanley wrote, "about nine inches in length and four in width, somewhat resembling a drowned rat."

Doctors in town told Thompson they could sew the scalp back to his head. They couldn't. After a painful failure of an operation, Thompson donated his scalp to the Omaha Public Library (where it was put on display in the children's section).

The Plum Creek attack became famous thanks to Thompson's incredible survival story. But it was just one of a growing number of Indian raids on railroad workers. "We have had a very anxious day of it," a UP worker named Arthur Ferguson wrote in his diary. "On the lookout from morning until night, not knowing but what we might be attacked at every turn of the road."

The men running the Union Pacific demanded action from the government. "We've got to clean the damn Indians out, or give up building the Union Pacific," grumbled Grenville Dodge, the railroad's chief engineer. "The government may make its choice."

No Interruptions Allowed

It was an easy choice to make. The government considered the railroad far too important to allow anything, or anyone, to stand in its way. General William Tecumseh Sherman summed up the government's tough stand:

"No interruption to the work upon the line

of the Union Pacific will be tolerated. Both the

Sioux* and Cheyenne must die, or submit."

William Tecumseh Sherman

* *another name for Lakota*

While helping lead the Union army to victory in the Civil War, Sherman had gained a reputation for his merciless fighting style. "War is cruelty," he was famous for saying. "The crueler it is, the sooner it will be over." In other words: *War sucks, so you might as well get it over with. Don't just attack enemy armies—burn their homes, destroy their farms, break their will, force them to give up.*

Sherman's strategy had worked against the South. It would work on the Great Plains too. "You should not allow the troops to settle down on the defensive," he told his generals, "but carry the war to the Indian camps, where the women and children are." Soldiers attacked villages in winter, burning food supplies and driving survivors out into the snow. The Cheyenne, the Arapaho, and other groups living in the path of railroad had no choice—they agreed to move onto reservations further to the south.

Red Cloud Wins One

Then the United States turned its attention to ending Red Cloud's War, which was still dragging on north of the railroad route. Here the government did something surprising: it admitted defeat. Soldiers abandoned forts along the Bozeman Trail. The road was closed.

Lakota chiefs then agreed to make peace, signing the Fort Laramie Treaty of 1868. "The government of the United States desires peace, and its honor is hereby pledged to keep it," declared the treaty. "The Indians desire peace, and they now pledge their honor to maintain it."

The Fort Laramie Treaty created what was called the Great Sioux

Reservation. This was a massive chunk (about eighteen million acres) of traditional Lakota land that was forever off-limits to American travelers and settlers. At least, it was supposed to be.

For the first time in American history Native American tribes had beaten the United States in a war. Government officials didn't seem too upset, though. For them, the real key was protecting the transcontinental railroad. Sherman's soldiers started guarding the railroad workers as they laid tracks across the Plains.

But would this railroad ever actually be completed?

California Update

No, judging by the progress of the Central Pacific in California. We haven't checked in on them in a while. We haven't missed much—the CP still needed thousands of workers.

Here's where the Chinese immigrants come back into the story. By the early 1860s nearly 50,000 Chinese immigrants had arrived in California, almost all of them young men. Chased off the good gold mining spots and forced to pay bogus taxes, they had little chance of making money as miners. They were eager for work— any work.

Charles Crocker (another of the Big Four; weight: 265 pounds) thought it made sense to hire some of these men.

"I will not boss Chinese!" shouted James Strobridge, boss of the CP's construction crews.

"But who said laborers have to be white to build railroads?" asked Crocker.

"I was very much prejudiced against Chinese labor," Strobridge later admitted.

Crocker convinced Strobridge to try just fifty Chinese workers. "They did so well that he took fifty more," Crocker reported, "and he got more and more until finally we got all we could use, until at one time I think we had ten or twelve thousand."

By 1866, Chinese workers (ranging in age from thirteen to sixty) made up about 80 percent of the Central Pacific's entire workforce. True, they had some habits that white workers found weird. They bathed a lot, for example. They sent to San Francisco for seaweed, dried fish, and vegetables, and they drank only tea. Turns out they knew what they were doing. Boiling water for tea killed germs. And the varied diet of fresh food kept them much healthier than other workers, who ate plate after plate of meat and potatoes, sloshed down with muddy water scooped from the nearest stream.

So the Central Pacific had itself a good workforce. But as the men built their way east, they ran smack into the question that had faced Theodore Judah: Was it even possible to build a railroad over the rugged peaks of the Sierra Nevada?

Blasting Through the Mountains

Actually, no.

But, with enough courage and patience, it might be possible to build tracks through the mountains—literally *through* them. Teams of Chinese workers got the job of carving tunnels through mountains of solid granite. Workers would stand at the top of a cliff and lower other men over the edge on long ropes. Using hand drills, these guys would slowly drill small holes into the side of the mountain. They filled the holes with gunpowder, lit fuses, then jerked on the ropes—the signal for the men on top to pull them up as quickly as possible.

Historians haven't been able to find any letters or journals written by Chinese workers on the Central Pacific. But a worker named Wong Hau-hon, who helped build railroads in Canada in the 1880s, described the process of blasting through solid rock. "The work was very dangerous," he said. The men were under constant pressure to work very quickly, which made the job even riskier. While blasting one tunnel, workers were sent back in before all the gunpowder had exploded.

"Just at that moment the remaining two charges suddenly exploded," said Wong Hau-hon. "Chinese bodies flew from the cave

as if shot from a cannon. Blood and flesh were mixed in a horrible mess." At least ten men died that day, he reported. We know that accidents like this took the lives of Central Pacific workers as well.

Even with the men taking these terrible risks, progress was painfully slow. "We are only averaging about one foot per day," complained Charles Crocker.

Then came the snowstorms—workers counted more than forty of them during the winter of 1866–67. At first the men shoveled the snow off the tracks, dumping it into empty train cars. When cars overflowing with snow rolled into Sacramento (where it hardly ever snows), cheering children raced to the train and started a massive snowball fight.

Up in the mountains the snow kept falling, drifting into piles more than sixty feet high. Rather than quit for the winter, workers dug tunnels down to the tracks and continued working under the snow. The tunnels had stairs and rooms and even blacksmith shops. But the bitter cold and the constant threat of avalanches made them

deadly places to work. Central Pacific records include reports that say things such as:

"Snow slides carried away our camps and we lost a good many men."

"Some fifteen or twenty Chinese were killed by a [snow] slide about this time."

"A good many were frozen to death."

As you can tell from these reports, the Central Pacific never bothered to count the exact number of Chinese workers killed on the job. It was certainly somewhere in the hundreds, maybe even the thousands.

"We Are Now Sailing"

The Union Pacific was having a better time. *Possibly too good,* thought Frances Casement. Like Americans everywhere, she was following the railroad race in her daily newspaper. The more she read, the more she worried. She wrote to her husband, Jack, who was in charge of construction crews for the Union Pacific, saying: "Dear Jack, Do get home as soon as possible—and darling, be careful of your health—and for the sake of our little boy more than for your own sake, beware of the tempter in the form of strong drink."

Frances had been reading stories about the wild towns springing up along the railroad tracks. As soon as railroad workers arrived in a new spot, other folks rushed in to set up bars and gambling houses. Some came simply to steal. "There are men here who would murder a fellow creature for five dollars," reported one journalist in a Nebraska town. "Nay," he added, "there are men who have already done it." A newspaper in another town along the tracks actually ran a daily column called "Last Night's Shootings." (They weren't all shootings: in

Paint Rock, Nebraska, two girls killed their sleeping stepmother by pouring melted lead into her ear.)

All of this helped sell newspapers, but none of it slowed down the speeding Union Pacific. Jack Casement worked his men hard all day, then lit bonfires along the tracks and had other crews work all night. "We are now sailing," he reported, "and mean to lay over three miles every day."

General Sherman was working hard to protect workers from Indian attacks—and the Union Pacific was working hard to keep Sherman happy. A UP official named Herbert Hoxie told Sherman that the railroad had decided to name a water station in his honor. (Trains stopped at these stations to fill up on water, which was needed to run the steam engines.) This conversation followed:

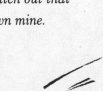

Sherman: *Where is it?*

Hoxie: *[pointing to a map] Down here in Nebraska.*

Sherman: *Oh, I don't want a water station named after me. Why, nobody will live there. Where is the highest point on the road?*

Hoxie: *Altamont.*

Sherman: *Just scratch out that name, and put down mine.*

And that's how Sherman, Wyoming—the station at the highest elevation along the Union Pacific—got its name. (Sherman might be sad to know it's a ghost town today.)

The CP Starts Sailing Too

In 1868 the Central Pacific workers finally finished what many had said was impossible—they busted through the mountains of California. Suddenly the CP started to pick up speed as it built tracks across the flat Nevada desert.

In need of extra hands to keep the work cruising along, the railroad hired Paiute and Shoshone workers. This actually caused a brief delay when some of the Indians told Chinese workers that out in the desert ahead slithered enormous snakes that swallowed men whole. It was meant as a joke, of course. But these Chinese crews had seen enough danger for ten lifetimes, and a few hundred of the men decided it was time to head back to San Francisco. Other Central Pacific workers had to ride after them and plead with them to come back to work.

To the Central Pacific's Big Four, speed was everything now. They were determined to build as quickly as possible and collect as much money as possible—even if it meant building tracks that would soon fall apart. "The line we construct now is the one we can build the soonest, even if we rebuild immediately," said one CP engineer.

Didn't this present a problem when government inspectors came to look at the quality of the track? Not really, said a *San Francisco Chronicle* reporter named W. H. Rhodes, who watched one of these government inspections in Nevada. Rhodes noticed that whenever the train stopped for water, the CP's Charles Crocker handed out another round of whiskey to the government inspectors. "In truth we became hilarious," reported Rhodes (*hilarious* was nineteenth-century slang for "really drunk").

One of the inspectors soon fell asleep face-down on the floor of the train. Crocker insisted that the man could continue his inspection that way: "If the passengers could sleep, the track must be level, easy, and all right; whereas, if too rough to sleep, something must be wrong with the work." The inspector was able to stay asleep. When he woke up, he gave his official approval to the tracks, and the government money continued rolling in.

Sprint to the Finish Line

The Union Pacific was doing the same thing—building crummy track as quickly as possible. To keep the tracks moving during winter, UP workers even built tracks on top of ice!

Work crews for both companies started speeding through Utah in 1869. In fact, they sped right past each other. Eager to build as many miles of track as possible, the two companies went right past the meeting point and starting building railroads right next to each other in opposite directions.

Realizing that the race was getting ridiculous (and expensive), Congress forced the heads of the two companies to pick a spot for the rails to meet. They agreed to join their tracks at Promontory Summit, Utah. This made the final track-building score:

Union Pacific: *1,086 miles of track from Omaha to Promontory Summit*

Central Pacific: *690 miles of track from Sacramento to Promontory Summit*

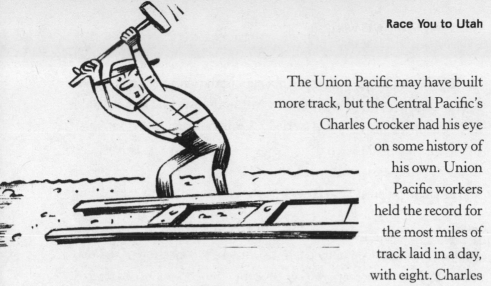

The Union Pacific may have built more track, but the Central Pacific's Charles Crocker had his eye on some history of his own. Union Pacific workers held the record for the most miles of track laid in a day, with eight. Charles Crocker announced that his men would beat the record. But he wanted to make sure that once he set the record it would stay set. "We must not beat them until we get so close together that there is not enough room for them to turn around and outdo me," Crocker told his construction boss, James Strobridge.

"How are you going to do it?" Strobridge asked.

"I have been thinking over this for two weeks and I have it all planned," Crocker said.

Crocker waited until his men reached the flat stretch of land close to Promontory Summit. He promised his Chinese and Irish work crews four days' wages if they could build ten miles of track in a day. *No problem*, they told him.

Beginning before sunrise on April 28, the well-organized teams finished six miles by lunchtime. They took an hour lunch break, then built another four miles and fifty-six feet of good-quality track by sundown. (The most amazing thing about the ten-mile day: just one eight-man team lifted every single seven-hundred-pound iron rail used that day—meaning each man carried 2.1 million pounds of iron.)

The Golden Spike

On the sunny spring morning of May 10, 1869, people gathered at Promontory Point, Utah, to witness the meeting of the two railroads. Newspaper reporters got out their notebooks, bands started warming up, and liquor sellers set up tents by the tracks. "Everyone had all they wanted to drink all the time," said Alexander Toponce, who was there on the historic day. "I do not remember what any of the speakers said, but I do remember that there was a great abundance of champagne."

Union Pacific officials almost missed the party, since a few of their badly built bridges had already collapsed. Several times the officials had to get out of their train, trip past broken sections of track, then get on a new train and continue west. They finally made it to Promontory, where they watched a Chinese team lay the final rail connecting the two railroads. A specially made spike of gold was set in place. On the spike was the inscription "May God continue the unity of our country as this railroad unites the two great oceans of the world."

At this moment a telegraph operator named Watson Shilling became the most important person in America. Huge crowds in cities all over the country were waiting to explode with excitement the moment the railroad was completed. Shilling sat by the tracks, ready to send out the news.

"Almost ready," Shilling tapped out to the waiting nation. "Hats off. Prayer is being offered."

A few minutes later, an update: "We have got done praying. The spike is about to be presented."

Then: "All ready now, the spike will soon be driven."

Then the Central Pacific's Leland Stanford stepped forward with a hammer. The plan was for him to tap the golden spike, just for show. He lifted the heavy hammer over his shoulder, and . . .

"He missed the spike and hit the rail," Toponce reported. "What a howl went up! Irish, Chinese, Mexicans, and everybody yelled with delight. 'He missed it. Yee!'"

Then Thomas Durant of the Union Pacific took a try. "And he missed the spike the first time," said Toponce. "Then everybody slapped everybody else again and yelled, 'He missed it too, yow!'"

Leland Stanford

Other witnesses didn't report Stanford and Durant swinging and missing, so we can't be sure if it really happened. We do know that somewhere in there, the telegraph operator got tired of waiting and tapped out the one-word message the entire nation was waiting for:

"Done."

This set off wild all-day and all-night parties from New York City to San Francisco. Cannons blasted, fireworks boomed. Fire alarms and church bells rang, and people started singing and dancing and making speeches. Most Americans had nothing to do with building the transcontinental railroad, but they still took a huge amount of pride in the project. No other country had ever built anything like it. Americans sensed that their nation had just taken a major step toward becoming a great power in the world. As one Union Pacific worker at Promontory proudly put it: "The future is coming, and fast too."

Sitting at home in Massachusetts, Theodore Judah's wife, Anna, joined the celebration in her own quiet way. "The spirit of my brave husband descended upon me," she said, "and together we were there unseen."

Early Train Travelers (and Robbers)

Americans could now cross the nation in eight to ten days—a fact that seemed absolutely amazing in 1869. "Every man who could command the time and money was eager to make the trip," wrote one reporter.

Early journeys often didn't go smoothly. First of all, both the Union Pacific and Central Pacific were still busy working on the tracks, rebuilding all the sections of rail they had built too quickly the first time. Also, no one had really figured out how things like meals should work. The train didn't serve food. Instead, it stopped at stations along the track and hungry passengers tumbled out and rushed into nearby dining halls. Knowing the train would leave again in half an hour, everyone shouted at once:

"Steak!"

"Coffee!"

"Bread!"

"Trout!"

"Waiter, a napkin!"

In addition to the stress of getting back to the train on time, a traveler named Susan Coolidge noticed that every place she went served the exact same thing. "It was necessary to look at one's watch to tell whether it was breakfast, dinner, or supper we were eating." she said.

As the train headed farther west, riders ran into a kind of culture clash. Wealthy riders from eastern cities suddenly found themselves sharing train cars with pistol-packing miners who spat tobacco juice on the floor. The miners turned out to be friendly, though, often holding out bottles of whiskey to the fancy folks and saying, "Smile?" (western slang for "Have a drink?").

Slightly less friendly were the men who pulled off the West's first major train robbery. It all began on the morning of November 4, 1870, when A. J. Davis got a telegram from a friend in Oakland, California:

"Send me sixty dollars and charge to my account.
—J. Enrique"

This was the coded message Davis was waiting for. It meant that a Central Pacific train had just left Oakland, heading west with $60,000.

At midnight, when the train slowed down to pass through the town of Verdi, Nevada, Davis and four other men in black masks jumped on board. They unhooked the engine car and express car (which had the money boxes) from the rest of the train. These first two cars continued on, while the other cars, full of snoring passengers, drifted quietly back along the tracks.

Davis and the gang busted into the engine car and pulled their guns on the engineer, Henry Small. They told him to drive on a bit, then made him stop at a dark spot. They ordered him to knock on the door of the express car.

"Who's there?" the guard asked.

With a gun sticking in his back, the engineer was forced to say, "Small."

Recognizing the voice, the guard opened the door. The robbers charged in, cracked the money boxes with crowbars, filled their bags with twenty-dollar gold

coins, hopped onto horses they'd hidden along the tracks, and rode off in separate directions.

Henry Small, meanwhile, drove his engine car back to the rest of train and reattached the other cars. The passengers were still asleep. They had no idea anything had happened.

So the first train robbery was a success—though a short-lived one. Over the following weeks the robbers were all tracked down and arrested. The stolen gold was recovered, except for about 150 coins, which the thieves must have buried somewhere along the Truckee River. (People in Nevada are still searching for that stash—it's worth over a half a million dollars today.)

Red Cloud Goes to Washington

Another early traveler on the transcontinental railroad was Red Cloud, the Lakota chief who had recently won his war against American forces.

In 1870 U.S. government officials invited Red Cloud to come to Washington, D.C. They wanted to talk to him about how to preserve the fragile peace between settlers and Indians in the West. Red Cloud and fifteen other Lakota leaders boarded a Union Pacific train and headed east through Omaha, Chicago, and on to Washington. There they were met by the government's commissioner of Indian affairs, a Seneca Indian named Ely Parker.

"I am very glad to see you here today," Parker said. "I want to hear what Red Cloud has to say for himself and his people."

But Red Cloud was tired from the long trip. "Telegraph to my people and say that I am safe," he told Parker. "That is all I have to say today."

Red Cloud and the other Indians were taken to an expensive hotel, where their huge suites were furnished with pitchers of lemonade and baskets of oranges, nuts, and cigars. The next day they were given fancy American suits (which they found terribly tight and uncomfortable) and went to the Capitol building to watch senators make speeches (which they found terribly boring). A photographer asked permission to take Red Cloud's picture, but he refused, saying, "I am not dressed for such an occasion." He didn't want anyone photographing him in the ridiculous suit.

Then they went on to the White House to have dinner with President Ulysses S. Grant. The Lakota chief Spotted Tail particularly loved the strawberry ice cream. "Surely the white men have many more good things to eat than they send to the Indians," he commented.

When everyone finally got down to business, Ely Parker

explained that the United States was committed to living peacefully with the Plains Indians. Red Cloud agreed with this goal and thought it should be easy to achieve. "The white children have surrounded me and left me nothing but an island," Red Cloud said. Let the Lakota keep this island of land, he explained, and there will be no more war.

Next Red Cloud stopped off in New York City, where crowds of people lined the streets and cheered as he rode past on a horse. "We want to keep the peace," Red Cloud told New Yorkers. "Will you help us?"

Red Cloud understood—now more clearly than ever—that he would need help. The trip gave him a close-up view of busy American factories and enormous American cities. There was simply no way he and his warriors could continue winning wars against such a massive and growing nation.

So Red Cloud headed home a bit depressed. And it could not have helped his mood to see so many trains packed with people racing west. He must have been wondering: *Where are all these people going? How long until they start crowding onto our land?*

Speaking of Heading West . . .

One of those heading west was Nat Love, a teenager who had grown up in slavery in Tennessee. "I was at that time about fifteen years old," he said of the moment he left home.

"And though while young in years, the hard work and farm life had made me strong and hearty, much beyond my years, and I had full confidence in myself as being able to take care of myself and making my way."

Nat Love

Love traveled west to Dodge City, Kansas, a booming town along the railroad. What was there to see in town? "A great many saloons, dance halls, and gambling houses," Love said, "and very little of anything else."

But Love did see one thing that interested him: cowboys. Even more interesting was that many of them were African American. Love decided to find out exactly what these guys did for a living. The cowboys told him that they had spent the last few months leading a huge herd of cattle from Texas all the way here to Dodge City. They were about to head home to Texas to do it all over again. Love decided he'd like to join them, and went to find the boss of the crew.

"Can you ride a wild horse?" the boss asked.

"Yes, sir," Love responded.

"If you can I will give you a job."

The boss pointed out a horse named Good Eye, the wildest horse he had. He told Love to jump on. As Love approached the horse, a cowboy named Bronco Jim warned him that the horse would probably send him flying.

"I told Jim I was a good rider and not afraid," Love said.

The cowboys crowded around, eager to watch Good Eye toss this skinny kid into the air.

Cowboys vs. Farmers

Fifteen-year-old Nat Love swung up onto Good Eye, and his cowboy tryout began with a jolt. "This proved the worst horse to ride I had ever mounted in my life," he said. The huge beast twisted and kicked, but Love somehow stayed in the saddle. When Good Eye finally tired, Love jumped off—and saw surprise in the eyes of the watching cowboys. "They had taken me for a tenderfoot, pure and simple," Love said.

From then on, Nat Love was a cowboy.

Cowboys Wanted

Nat Love came to Kansas in 1869. It was a good time to get into the cowboy business.

The long and bloody Civil War had ended just four years before. When soldiers from Texas came home, they found huge herds of cattle wandering around the state. No one had been paying much attention to them during the war. Now there were millions of them.

Texans like steak, but they couldn't eat five million cows. And when you have a lot more of something than people want to buy, the price goes way down. In fact, cattle were worth only about three or four dollars each in Texas.

But remember, at this exact time, new railroads were being built across the country. This gave Texans an idea: Suppose we can get our cattle north to those railroads? Then trains can carry them east to busy cities, where cows are worth forty dollars each!

There was clearly money to be made. The challenge was getting the animals north to the railroad. That was the job of the cowboys.

Long Days on the Trail

"I was the poorest, sickliest little kid you ever saw," said a cowboy named Teddy Abbott. "All eyes, no flesh on me whatever."

When Abbott was ten years old, his father decided to let him help drive a herd of cattle north from Texas. "The idea was it would be good for my health," Abbott remembered. And it was. He spent the next few years outdoors, riding horses and roping cattle. "Those

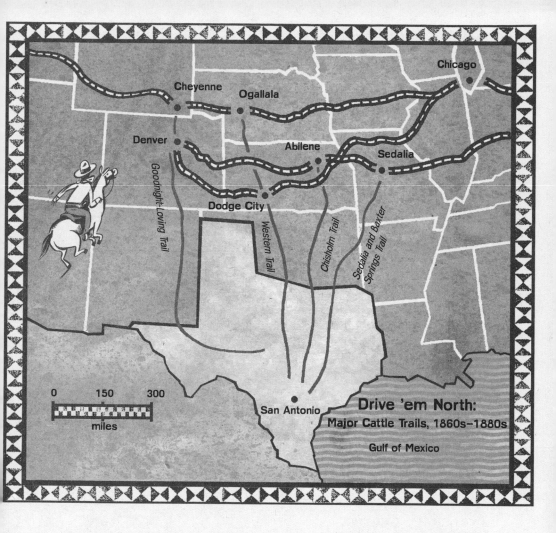

Cheyenne

Ogallala

Chicago

Denver

Abilene

Sedalia

Goodnight-Loving Trail

Dodge City

Western Trail

Chisholm Trail

Sedalia and Baxter Springs Trail

0   150   300
miles

San Antonio

Drive 'em North:
Major Cattle Trails, 1860s–1880s

Gulf of Mexico

years were what made a cowboy of me," said Abbott. "Nothing could have changed me after that." When he turned eighteen, Abbott left home to become a full-time cowboy.

Like Abbott, most cowboys were young men from the South. They were a diverse bunch, including many African Americans, Mexicans, and Native Americans. Skill was more important than skin color—and so was size. "The cowboys were mostly medium-sized men," Abbott explained. "A heavy man was hard on horses."

For a long cattle drive, ranchers would hire about six cowboys for every one thousand head of cattle. Spending seventeen-hour days on their horses, the cowboys surrounded the cattle and kept them moving north. They did this every day, seven days a week, for three or four months.

"We had no tents or shelter of any sort other than our blankets," one cowboy said about life on the trail. "Should anyone become injured, wounded, or sick, he would be strictly 'out of luck.' A quick recovery and a sudden death were the only desirable alternatives in such cases, for much of the time the outfit would be far from the settlements and from medical or surgical aid."

And there were plenty of ways to get hurt: poisonous snakes, rushing rivers that drowned cows and men, sudden storms of hail or lightning (Teddy Abbot was actually hit by lightning twice). But the thing cowboys feared most of all was a stampede, when herds of cattle suddenly panicked and started running wildly. These were naturally nervous animals. Almost any sudden sound could set off a stampede. A thunderclap, a gunshot, a coyote's yelp—even the clank of the cook's iron pots banging together—could send the cattle running. This made nights the most dangerous time for cowboys.

Long Nights Too

"**I**magine, my dear reader, riding your horse at the top of his speed through torrents of rain and hail, and darkness so black that we could not see our horses' heads, chasing an immense herd of maddened cattle, which we could hear but could not see, except during the vivid flashes of lightning, which furnished our only light."

That was Nat Love's frightening description of a night stampede. Even when it was too dark to see, Love and the boys had to jump onto their horses and chase down the speeding eight-hundred-pound animals. The stomping cattle could easily trample each other—and cowboys too. After one night's stampede, Teddy Abbott had the job of searching for a missing cowboy. "We found him among the prairie dog holes, beside his horse," Abbott said. "The horse's ribs were scraped bare of hide, and all the rest of horse and man was mashed into the ground as flat as a pancake."

Cowboys discovered that the best way to keep cattle calm at night was to sing to them. "The singing was supposed to soothe them, and it did," Abbott remembered. Two cowboys would ride along either side of the herd, taking turns singing back and forth. They soon got so sick of the songs they knew that they started making up new ones. Here's a sample from "The Old Chisholm Trail":

> *I'm up in the mornin' afore daylight*
> *And afore I sleep the moon shines bright*
> *Oh, it's bacon and beans most every day—*
> *I'd as soon be a-eatin' prairie hay . . .*

So after spending all day in the saddle, cowboys had to take a two-hour shift of singing every night. On a good night, they might get

four hours of sleep. "When you add it all up, I believe the worst hardship we had on the trail was loss of sleep," said Teddy Abbott. "Sometimes we would rub tobacco juice in our eyes to keep awake. It was rubbing them with fire."

If cowboys and their herds survived all of this—and they usually did—they made it north to the railroad lines by the end of summer. The plains were covered with thick grass, so there was plenty for the cattle to eat until the cowboys could sell them.

But the cowboys weren't the only ones who wanted to use this land.

What Are Farmers Doing Here?

In 1870 a ten-year-old boy named Percy Ebbutt, along with his father, older brother, and three family friends, sailed from Britain to the United States. They shared a dream: to start their own farm on the American Great Plains. The group traveled west by train, then bounced across the plains in a wagon to their new land in Kansas. "Of course, boy-like, I was looking forward to our life on the prairie as being all play or adventure," Ebbutt remembered.

There was plenty of adventure, but not so much play. After

unloading all their clothes and supplies, they broke up the wooden crates and built a tiny, shaky shack. Then one of the men tried to cook supper.

> *"Harry Parker made his first attempt at bread-baking, but was not*
>
> *over successful. The bread was baked in a great iron pan, and was*
>
> *as hard as a well-done brick, and*
>
> *about as digestible."*

**Percy
Ebbutt**

Men chopped off chunks with an ax. Then they turned to a much more troubling topic. "None of us knew anything whatever of farming," Ebbutt said. What made this family decide to cross an ocean to take on the enormous challenge of starting a farm? That's easy: there was lots of land available on the Great Plains, and it was cheap.

Up until recently, no one had thought of the dry, treeless plains as good farmland. Maps of the time actually labeled this vast region "the Great American Desert." That had started changing after the government passed the Homestead Act in 1862. This law said that any U.S. citizen twenty-one or older, or any immigrant who was in the process of becoming a citizen, could claim 160 acres of land on the Plains. You had to pay a ten-dollar filing fee, and you had to live and work on your property for five years. Then the land was yours.

The Homestead Act made it easy to get land. Maybe too easy. Families raced west to claim their land—but it takes a lot more than land to make a successful farm. You need money to buy seeds, farm equipment, animals, and food for your family while you're waiting for your first harvest. And of course, it helps to know how to actually run a farm.

Many homesteaders (or pioneers, as they came to be known) figured this out the hard way. Percy Ebbutt later warned potential homesteaders: "If you have made up your mind to go, you must also make up your mind to rough it." But stories about "roughing it" didn't scare people away from claiming homesteads on the Great Plains. For thousands of families, this was their one chance to get land of their own.

It was only after arriving on the Plains that they realized what "roughing it" really meant.

Roughing It, Pioneer Style

Martha Wooden took a train west to join her husband and sons, who had already claimed a piece of Kansas land. Martha's husband met her at the train station and they rode in a wagon toward their claim, which was about forty miles away. She gazed out at the flat grassy land stretching to the horizon in every direction. She didn't see a single tree or house all day. Then it started to get dark. She noticed her husband looking a little concerned. He stopped the wagon.

"Well, I guess I'm lost," he announced.

"Lost!" she said. "Out here on this lonely prairie?" Then she heard a loud howl.

"And what is that?" she asked.

"Oh, I guess you hear the coyotes."

Martha's husband got out of the wagon with a lantern, and she drove slowly behind him as they searched for their land. That was Martha Wooden's introduction to pioneer life.

There was a good reason Wooden didn't see any houses that first day: many newcomers didn't have the time or materials to build them. When a young pioneer named Howard Ruede arrived in Kansas, for example, he did what many others did—he got out his shovel and started digging. In a land with no trees, the quickest way to build a shelter was to dig one in the ground. "I tell you it is no easy work," Ruede reported to his family in Pennsylvania.

Ruede's six-foot-deep "dugout" was a good temporary solution, though it had its drawbacks. "It's awful hot," he wrote from the floor of his new home.

"The sweat runs off of me, and some of the drops wet the paper; so if you can't read it, you'll know the reason."

Howard Ruede

A teenage girl described another problem with having dirt walls and a grass roof. "Sometimes the bull snakes would get in the roof, and now and then one would lose his hold and fall down on the bed," she said. Then someone would have to grab a hoe, fight the snake, and toss it outside.

While sitting around drinking coffee one morning, another group of pioneers had a different sort of animal encounter. After pouring himself another cup, one of the men noticed something strange in the bottom of the pot. He turned to his friend Jim.

"Where'd you get that egg in the bottom of the coffeepot, Jim?"

"There's no egg," Jim said.

"But I can see an egg."

Jim took the coffeepot, turned it upside down, and out plopped a dead frog, swollen to several times its normal size. The men shrugged, then did what they did every morning: they started a long, hard day of work.

Roughing It, Continued

Before farmers could plant crops, they had to rip up the sod—thick grass with tangled roots reaching deep into the ground. It was backbreaking work, as Percy Ebbutt discovered. "The land that has been growing grass for centuries is one mass of roots," he said, "and the plough goes pop! pop! pop! cutting through them." The good news was the sod came up in heavy, foot-thick slabs of grass, roots, and dirt. Pioneers realized they could cut the sod into squares and use them like bricks to build new houses.

Sure, sod houses were full of bugs and snakes. Sure, they were dark, smoky, and always dusty. But they were cool in summer, warm in winter, and fireproof, and they lasted about ten years. Besides, families didn't come out here because they thought it was going to be easy. "There was running water in our sod house," joked a Nebraska homesteader. "It ran through the roof." When the roof of her sod house leaked (and they all did), one woman simply had her daughter hold an umbrella over the stove while she cooked. Another put her children to sleep under the table, where it was drier.

After getting the seeds into the ground, farmers faced the challenge of finding water. That usually meant digging a well. But how did you know where to dig? You didn't—unless you believed in "water witches," who claimed they could use a special stick to find underground water.

Howard Ruede had no cash to spend on magic sticks. He and his brother "Bub" got out picks and shovels, picked a spot, and started swinging. "But I had hardly made a dozen strokes before I struck myself on the head with the pick," Ruede said.

"It's bleeding, how!" Bub yelled.

"And sure enough it was!" remembered Ruede. "I bled like a stuck pig for a few minutes."

Howard and Bub chopped several twenty-five-foot holes in the earth, always striking dry stone at the bottom. "We'll have to go to another place to dig now," Ruede told his brother after each failure. Finally, after many exhausting weeks, they hit water.

Women pioneers, meanwhile, were working at least as hard—cleaning, cooking, making and mending clothes, planting gardens, watching young children, and taking care of farm animals. And everything was tougher out here on the open plains. "What could we burn for fuel?" wondered one newcomer. "There was not a tree, not even a bush, in sight."

She soon learned that dried buffalo and cow chips burned well enough for cooking. A Nebraska newspaper reported that women who were new to the plains would lift the brown blobs between two sticks. When they got a bit more used to the task, they used a rag instead. A bit later they used their apron. Finally they just picked up the chips with their bare hands, brushing their palms quickly on their skirt before turning to the next job.

Indians and Cowboys

In their letters and journals, women often wrote that the greatest hardship of pioneer life was loneliness. They had left behind parents and friends and hometowns (probably forever, they knew) and found themselves living in dirt houses in the middle of nowhere. Men at least got to travel to nearby towns for supplies once in a while. But women were always stuck at home. Looking out at the endless world of grass, listening to the whistling wind that reminded them of the emptiness all around . . . many women honestly feared they would lose their minds.

These were the times that the fear of Indians was greatest. A young pioneer named Grace Hays grew up hearing terrifying stories about Indian wars in the West. Her mother was always afraid of an Indian attack. And sometimes a few Native Americans really would suddenly show up at their door. "Of course, these Indians were friendly," she remembered, "almost too much so."

By 1870 the government had pushed most of the Indians of the eastern Great Plains onto reservations. The main danger between settlers and Indians was of cultural misunderstanding, not violence. Plains Indians simply had a different idea of privacy—they considered it perfectly normal to walk into a stranger's home and start looking around at the clothes and pots and food.

Mathilda Peterson was home alone one day, frying donuts in her Nebraska cabin, when a small group of Indians strolled in and sat down on the floor. They sat there quietly, watching her work, sniffing the sweet air. Feeling a bit nervous, Peterson dropped a donut and it rolled, still-sizzling, toward one of the guests. He picked it up and popped it his mouth. Judging by the expression on his face, he had never tasted anything so delicious. Peterson spent the next hour cooking donuts, serving batch after batch to her unexpected guests.

At her homestead in Kansas, a teenage pioneer named Jennie Marcy got a very different sort of surprise visit. She and her mother were working inside one day when the usual quiet was interrupted by a distant rumbling. The sound was getting louder and louder. She ran outside.

"I saw with my own two eyes that something was about to happen," Jennie said. "For down the road not far from the little prairie home were a thousand cattle."

No Love Lost

Jennie looked around for Pete, the family's watchdog. She found him snoring in the shade. She woke him up and pointed toward the herd of cattle coming toward their farm.

"Then," she said, "as I clapped my hands sharply and yelled, 'Sic 'em! Sic 'em!' he bounded off immediately."

Pete got a closer look at the coming herd—and decided to get out of the way. The cattle charged through the fence surrounding the Marcys' farm, snapping the wooden rails into small splinters. Jennie's mother rushed into the yard, saw a cow charging toward her, and fainted. Jennie helped her mom into the house, then ran back outside.

"I quickly mounted my pony," she said. But there was nothing she could do. A thousand huge animals were now spread out all over the farm, calmly chomping the grass and chewing the crops.

This kind of thing was happening a lot in the 1870s. As one cowboy said: "There was scarcely a day when we didn't have a row with some settler." The problem was that cowboys and pioneers were both trying to use the same land. On one Kansas farm in 1874, a herd of cattle actually stampeded right over a dugout house, and a cow fell through roof and landed on the bed of the sleeping settler. (Amazingly, neither was hurt.)

Cowboys were used to letting their herds graze on the wide-open plains. Now they saw more and more farmers claiming parts of this land, plowing right across the cattle trails. "And then," complained the cowboy Teddy Abbott, "when the cattle got into their wheat or their garden patch, they would come out cussing and waving a shotgun and yelling for damages."

Settlers saw things differently, of course. They had claimed this land legally. So why should they stand by and watch cattle eat their grass, trample their crops, and bring diseases to their farm animals? There were plenty of angry arguments between farmers and cowboys—and occasional gunfights.

On one cattle drive Teddy Abbott and another cowboy rode right past a settler's cabin. "We looked in the window of a little house," Abbott remembered, "and inside the open window we saw two big, white pillows on a bed. . . . I leaned down from my horse and grabbed one of the pillows and he took the other, and we throwed them in the wagon. I still had mine when I was married." (Which, by the way, was twenty years later.)

"It was a dirty trick as I look at it now," Abbott confessed, "but there was no love lost between settlers and cowboys on the trail."

Cow Towns of the Wild West

And speaking of tension between settlers and cowboys . . .
The long cattle drives ended at towns along the railroad—places that became known as "cow towns." When cowboys reached these towns after months of hard living on the trail, they felt they deserved a little fun. "We all headed for Dodge City to have a good time," Nat Love said after one long drive. "And I assure you we had it."

First the cowboys collected their pay. Then they usually stopped off at the barber for a shave and haircut, then on to a store for new clothes. Then, as Love fondly recalled, the fun began: "While our money lasted we would certainly enjoy ourselves, in dancing, drinking, and shooting up the town."

One settler saw a strange sight while doing a bit of shopping. "A cowboy named 'Bum' rode his pony 'Babe' into the store," she said, "and with his revolver drawn, ordered the clerk to give 'Babe' all the candy she wanted. Needless to say, the clerk obeyed."

In another cow town, Teddy Abbott earned himself a new nickname. After having a few too many drinks in a theater one night, he tried to walk behind the stage. But his spur caught on the carpet, sending him tripping into the middle of an ongoing show. He froze. Everyone was staring at him.

"Well, I thought, if you're before an

audience you've got to do something,

so I grabbed a chair from one

of the musicians and

straddled it and bucked

it all around the stage,

yelling, 'Whoa, Blue!

Whoa, Blue!'"

Teddy "Blue" Abbott

The audience was dying with laughter ("Whoa, Blue!" was a cowboy expression at the time). "And when I went out of the theater that night I was 'Blue,'" Abbott said, "and Teddy Blue I have been for forty-five years."

To cowboys, this kind of stuff was all in good fun. "We're not near so bad as we're painted," one cowboy said. "We like to get up a little racket now and then, but it's all in play."

Send in the Law

Settlers disagreed. They preferred nice, peaceful, quiet towns. The citizens of many cow towns decided it was time to bring in lawmen tough enough to tame the streets.

This wasn't so easy. In Abilene, Kansas, the mayor couldn't find anyone to take the job of police chief. Experienced lawmen kept arriving from the East, taking one look at the wild saloons and gambling halls, and then hopping right back on the train. Finally a former police officer and boxer from New York City named Tom Smith agreed to give it a try.

When Smith announced that no one would be allowed to carry guns in town anymore, a couple of cowboys named Big Hank and Wyoming Frank immediately challenged him. They strolled toward Smith with pistols in their holsters. Everyone in the street dove for cover, expecting a gunfight. But Smith didn't reach for his weapon. Instead, he stepped up to the bigger men and punched them both really hard, knocking them to the dirt. That gave Smith the most valuable tool a western lawman could have: the reputation of a man not to be messed with.

Tom Smith kept the peace in Abilene for six months. Then he was shot and killed while trying to make an arrest. Desperate for a new police chief, city leaders turned to James "Wild Bill" Hickok. When he took the job in 1871, Hickok was already famous as a ruthless gunfighter—and a creative storyteller, as this exchange with a reporter shows:

> Reporter: *I say, Bill, or Mr. Hickok, how many men have you killed to your certain knowledge?*
>
> Hickok: *I would be willing to take my oath on the Bible tomorrow that I have killed over a hundred.*
>
> Reporter: *What made you kill all those men? Did you kill them without cause?*
>
> Hickok: *No, by heaven! I never killed one man without good cause.*

This was a wild exaggeration, not to mention an odd thing to brag about. But Hickok knew that magazines and novels were making gunfighters like him famous. He was just doing a bit of self-promotion.

The everyday life of a gunfighter was usually less exciting. As police chief in Abilene, Hickok spent most of this

James "Wild Bill" Hickok

time playing cards in the Long Branch Saloon. Then one day he heard gunshots outside. He ran out and saw cowboys celebrating the end of a cattle drive by firing into the air. One of them pointed a gun at Hickok. Hickok fired, and the man fell. Hickok then saw someone else running toward him. He turned and fired and didn't see—until it was too late—that it was his deputy, Michael Williams.

This is not at all what the city council of Abilene had in mind. They fired Hickok (who, friends said, never forgave himself for killing Williams).

The Farmers Keep Coming

Stories of shootouts in the street make the Wild West sound a lot wilder that it really was. Historians point out that in the 1870s there was probably more violence in a typical week in New York City than there was in an entire month on the Great Plains.

Anyway, an occasional gunfight was hardly going to scare settlers away from the fertile farmland of the plains. After coming to Kansas from Sweden, Olof Olsson wrote to friends back home, explaining why so many people were still heading west: "The advantage which America offers is not to make everyone rich at once without toil and trouble, but the advantage is that the poor, who will and are able to work, secure a large piece of good land almost without cost."

For Europeans who couldn't afford land at home, this was too good to resist. Hundreds of thousands of hopeful farmers poured in from Germany, Sweden, and Norway. One third of the entire population of Iceland moved to the Great Plains.

States actually competed with each other to attract these immigrant families. Kansas, Nebraska, and Minnesota were all eager to grab Mennonite farmers from Russia. Followers of this religious group were looking for a new home with religious freedom and good farmland. When they arrived in Kansas, an agent working for the state of Nebraska stepped in. "I stole the whole bunch," he boasted, "and carried them all by special train, free, to Lincoln, Nebraska."

Some stayed, though most went on to settle in Kansas. The important thing is that these Mennonite families brought a special type of wheat they had been growing on the dry Russian plains. This wheat thrived on the dry American plains too, helping turn the Great Plains into the most productive wheat-growing region in the world.

It's Not Getting Easier

But even while their crops thrived, pioneers on the plains still had to rough it.

Every season brought its own special horrors. With the spring came the threat of floods, tornadoes, and hailstorms. Summers could bring 100-plus-degree heat, along with droughts and burning-hot winds. When the grasses dried out in the fall, wild prairie fires were a constant danger. "It is a strange and terrible sight to see all the fields a sea of fire," said one Nebraska settler. "Quite often the scorching flames sweep everything along in their path—people, cattle, hay, fences."

Then came the long winters. Percy Ebbutt, the young pioneer from Britain, found no way to escape the cold. "While sitting round the red-hot stove at breakfast," he reported, "one's coffee would freeze in a very short time if placed on the table a few feet from the fire."

Like all successful pioneers, the Ebbutts found ways to adapt to the harsh conditions. If the temperature in your house is below freezing, for example, why not use it as a freezer? "We used to keep a pig in the house during the winter to cut from—a dead one," Ebbutt said. "It used to hang in one corner of the room over the flour barrel, and was frozen as hard as a board. We used just to take a hatchet and cut off as much as we wanted to fry."

The real danger in winter was getting stuck outside when a blizzard hit. Blizzard winds were so thick with blinding snow that farmers had no hope of finding their way home from their fields. The only way to survive was to slice open a horse and crawl into its guts for warmth. But the dead horse didn't stay warm for long—sometimes, after blizzards, men were found frozen to death inside their frozen animals.

And there was no way to adapt to the most terrifying threat of all, as farmers found out in the summer of 1874. There had been plenty of rain that spring. Farmers were looking forward to huge harvests—until the afternoon of August 1.

"There was not a hint of cloud in the sky," remembered one Kansas farmer. "Then the sky suddenly darkened."

Year of the Grasshopper

It seemed as if we were in a big snowstorm," Mary Lyon remembered. "The air was filled with enormous-size flakes." But who ever heard of a blizzard in August? Then Lyon realized her mistake. What looked like swirling snowflakes was actually the sparkle of sunlight bouncing off millions of flapping bug wings. She watched in horror as a sky-covering cloud of grasshoppers dropped down on her Kansas farm.

No one living on the Great Plains would ever forget the grasshopper invasion of 1874. Percy Ebbutt, now fourteen, had an experience similar to Mary Lyon's. "We first saw a glittering cloud high in the sky," he said. Then grasshoppers started plunking down to the ground, just one or two at a time at first. Overjoyed chickens gobbled the bugs as fast as they fell.

Then the hoppers started dropping in groups of thousands, landing on crops, trees, barns, houses, animals, people. One Kansas farmer said:

"The ground was covered, in some spots to a depth of three or four inches. Trees along the creek were so loaded that large limbs were broken off."

"It was impossible to walk about without killing dozens at each step," Percy Ebbutt recalled. Men tied strings around the bottom of their pants, hoping to stop the bugs from hopping into their underwear. There was no way to keep them off your hands or face. Still, farmers felt they had to get out there and do something to protect their crops.

"Go get your shawls, heavy dresses, and quilts!"

That's what a twelve-year-old girl named Lillie Marcks heard her father yelling when the grasshoppers landed on the family's farm. "We will cover the cabbage and celery beds," he said. "Perhaps we can save that much."

Lillie and her five-year-old sister charged out into the storm, swinging branches at the bugs and covering plants with any piece of clothing they could find. It was no use. The grasshoppers simply ate the clothes, then ate everything underneath. Swarms of hoppers chomped down fields of wheat, corn, melons, onions—even tobacco. They devoured entire bushes, leaving trees as leafless as they would have been in the middle of winter. When nothing green was left, the bugs started eating wooden fences and the handles of pitchforks.

Grasshoppers also fell into wells by the thousands. Percy Ebbutt had the disgusting job of climbing down his farm's well to try to keep them from ruining the water. "I would then take a small dipper or gourd," he said, "and skim all the hoppers into the bucket, which was drawn up and emptied by someone at the top."

The bugs kept coming back, though. Soon the water in wells and creeks all over the plains turned coffee brown with grasshopper droppings. And chickens and pigs ate so many bugs, their meat tasted like grasshopper.

The grasshopper invasion devastated farms all over the plains, from Texas in the south all the way north to the Dakotas. People in other parts of the nation collected donations of money and goods to send to farm families. But getting the stuff there was a challenge, since train tracks on the plains were coated with crushed bugs. The rails were so greasy with bug juice that train wheels spun helplessly in place, unable to grip the track.

Time for Teachers

Hardships like the grasshopper invasion drove many farmers away from the Great Plains. Still, the population of plains states continued growing steadily through the 1870s and 1880s.

As more and more people settled in this part of the country, communities started building schools for the local children. These early schoolhouses were often one-room sod shacks, with a stove in the back and blackboard in front. The students sat on long benches without backs, which was especially tough on the kids whose feet didn't reach the ground. "Little legs, dangling high in the air, would ache cruelly," one teacher remembered.

The teachers were mostly very young women, many as young as sixteen—teaching was one of the few jobs open to them at the time. Mollie Dorsey Sanford took over a schoolhouse in Nebraska when she was twenty. "I have twenty scholars, mostly young children," she wrote in her journal. "My children range from six to nine years, and of course the younger ones are restless! But I have won their love."

Since many young teachers were working far from home, local families took turns housing the teachers. The more kids a family had in school, the longer they were supposed to feed and house the teacher. For teachers, this meant they spent the longest amounts of time in the houses that were already the most crowded (and short on food).

Mollie Dorsey Sanford said the lack of privacy in one crowded cabin really started to bother her. So did the bugs. "At this place I slept on the floor," she wrote, "and festive bedbugs held high carnival over my weary frame the night through."

Are you starting to get the feeling there was no easy way to make a living in the West? That may be true—though a young man named Frank Mayer heard of a job that paid really well, at least.

The Road to Little Bighorn

In the early 1870s factories in the East started using buffalo hides to make leather for shoes, belts, and bags. The word spread west—hunters could make a fortune by bringing in buffalo hides. "They were walking gold pieces," Frank Meyer said of the buffalo. "I was young, twenty-two. I could shoot. I  liked to hunt. I needed adventure. Here was it. Wouldn't you have done the same thing if you had been in my place?"

Goodbye, Buffalo

There had been about thirty million buffalo in the West when white settlers started arriving. Now buffalo hunters started killing more than a million of them every year. They sometimes blasted buffalo so quickly that their rifles overheated and they had to urinate down the barrels to cool them off. After killing the animals, hunters stripped off the hides, leaving the bodies to rot in the sun.

Some hunters didn't even bother to take the hides. A woman named Elizabeth Custer got a close-up view of the buffalo slaughter while heading west by train to meet her husband, an officer in the army. "I have been on a train when the black, moving mass of buffaloes before us looked as if it stretched on down to the horizon," Custer said. As soon as passengers (the men, that is) spotted the herds, they yanked guns from their suitcases and stuck them out the windows of the moving train.

"It was the greatest wonder that more people were not killed," she said, "as the wild rush for the windows, and the reckless discharge of rifles and pistols, put every passenger's life in jeopardy."

The men considered this great fun (and like Custer said, only a few passengers got shot). To the Plains Indians, it was cruel and crazy.

"Everything the Kiowa had came from the buffalo," said one Kiowa woman. "Their tepees were made of buffalo hides, so were their clothes and moccasins. They ate buffalo meat. Their containers were made of hide, or of bladders or stomachs. The buffalo were the life of the Kiowa." The buffalo were just as important to the Cheyenne, Lakota, and other Plains Indians.

This actually explains why the U.S. government supported the work of buffalo hunters. Once there were no more buffalo to hunt, Plains Indians would no longer be able to roam freely across the plains. Unable to live their traditional way of life, they'd be forced to settle down on reservations.

As General William T. Sherman saw it, killing buffalo was a way of defeating the Plains Indians—and it was a lot easier (also cheaper and safer) than fighting the Indians directly. "Let them kill, skin, and sell until the buffalo is exterminated," Sherman said of buffalo hunters. "It is the only way to bring peace and allow civilization to advance."

It was a harsh strategy. And it was working. "The great buffalo slaughter commenced in the West," remembered the cowboy Nat Love. "And in 1877 they had become so scarce that it was a rare occasion when you came across a herd containing more than fifty animals, where before you could find thousands in a herd."

Sitting Bull and Hard Backsides

With the buffalo herds disappearing, more Plains Indians groups agreed to move onto reservations. But the Lakota chief Sitting Bull refused to even consider such a move.

As a young boy he had been known by the name Hunkesni, which means "slow." It wasn't an insult, exactly. It's just that he had a serious stubborn streak, doing everything at his own pace. By 1874, Sitting Bull was a respected chief in his early forties. He was still stubborn too: stubbornly convinced that his people had the right to continue to live free on their own land. As he said to Indians who had agreed to settle on reservations and live on food from the American government:

"The whites may get me at last, as you say, but I will have good times till then. You are fools to make yourselves slaves to a piece of fat bacon, some hard-tack, and a little sugar and coffee."

Sitting Bull

Sitting Bull was confident the Lakota could continue living in their traditional way—thanks to the huge Great Sioux Reservation, the territory won by the Lakota in Red Cloud's War. The Black Hills, in what is now South Dakota, were an especially rich hunting region of the Great Sioux Reservation. According the Fort Laramie Treaty between the Lakota and the U.S. government, this land belonged to the Lakota forever.

So what was the American army doing there? That's what Lakota leaders were wondering in the summer of 1874 (just eight years after the treaty was signed) as they watched an army officer named George Armstrong Custer lead one thousand American soldiers into the Black Hills. The Lakota knew Custer well—he was famous for his flowing blond hair and his aggressive battle style. Once, after chasing a group of warriors for hours without ever getting out of his saddle, the Lakota nicknamed him "Hard Backsides."

Custer claimed he was in the Black Hills just looking things over, making sure the Lakota were behaving themselves (not that he had any legal right to do that). The truth is, rumors were swirling about gold in those hills. Custer was ordered to go have a look.

"Our people knew there was yellow metal in little chunks up there," said a Lakota teenager named Black Elk. "But they did not bother with it, because it was not good for anything."

Custer did not agree. "We have discovered a rich and beautiful country," he wrote to his wife, Elizabeth (without explaining how you can "discover" a country where other people are already living). He was thrilled by the opportunity to add to his growing collection of western wildlife: "I have one live rattlesnake," he told Elizabeth, "two jack-rabbits, half-grown, one eagle, and four owls. I had also two fine badgers, full-grown, but they were accidentally smothered."

More important, Custer's soldiers squatted in streams to pan for gold. It was there, all right. "We have discovered gold without a doubt, and probably other valuable metals," he reported.

Sitting Bull watched Custer's army march out of the Black Hills and back toward American territory. There would be no fighting that summer. The Lakota just watched and waited and wondered what the Americans were really up to.

Black Hills: Not for Sale

They found out soon enough.

Custer's discovery was headline news all over the country. "Rich Mines of Gold and Silver Reported Found by Custer," announced one newspaper. This set off a new gold rush, with thousands of miners swarming into the Black Hills.

The American army was legally required to remove the miners. But the government decided it would be simpler just to buy the Black Hills. "You should bow to the wishes of the government," one senator told Lakota leaders. "Gold is useless to you, and there will be fighting unless you give it up."

When Sitting Bull heard the government was setting up a conference to work out a price for the Black Hills, he sent a message to President Grant. "I want you to go and tell the Great Father that I do not want to sell any land to the government," he told an interpreter. Picking up a pinch of dust, he added: "Not even as much as this."

The government officials came west anyway and tried negotiating with the few chiefs who were willing to talk. It did not go well. The government offered six million dollars for the Black Hills. Far too low a price, the chiefs responded. While the arguments flew back and forth, three hundred Lakota warriors rode up to the outdoor meeting. Holding rifles high in the air, they sang a new song specially written for the occasion:

> *The Black Hills is my land and I love it*
> *And whoever interferes*
> *Will hear this gun.*

The frustrated (and nervous) government men hurried back to Washington, D.C., to report their failure. At this point, President Grant and General Sherman decided they were done negotiating. They sent a warning to Sitting Bull and the other Lakota leaders: Report to reservations by January 31, 1876—or the army will come and bring you in.

Another Miserable Job

The job of actually going and getting the Lakota fell to American soldiers stationed in western forts. Here was yet another very tough way to make a living in the West.

Low-paid soldiers spent years stuck in small log forts, hundreds of miles from anywhere. The loneliness and boredom were unbearable. So was the food, which included case after case of moldy biscuits left over from the Civil War.

There were unexpected troubles too, as Martha Summerhayes discovered. Martha's husband, Jack, an army lieutenant, was assigned to a fort in the West. Like many officers' wives, she decided to go with him.

"Our sleeping room was very small," she said, "and its one window looked out over the boundless prairie at the back of the post." Summer nights were baking hot, and they had to sleep with their window wide open. Along with a slight breeze, this let in the growls of mountain lions. Nothing to worry about, her husband assured her.

One night the cat cries seemed a little closer. "I asked him if they ever came in," Martha remembered.

"Gracious, no!" Jack said. "They are too wild."

So she tried again to get comfortable in bed.

"I calmed myself for sleep—when like lightning,

one of the huge creatures gave a flying leap in at

our window, across the bed, and through into

the living-room."

"Jerusalem!" shouted Lieutenant Summerhayes.

He tumbled out of bed, grabbed his sword from the corner, and, swinging and stabbing wildly, chased the wild cat back into the bedroom, onto the bed, over Martha, and out the open window.

Nothing this exciting (or dangerous) usually happened in western forts. The two biggest health hazards in the forts were disease and alcohol abuse. Soldiers were often so bored that they welcomed the chance to march off toward battle.

That's exactly what happened in May 1876. The government's deadline had come and gone. Sitting Bull and most of the Lakota still refused to surrender. "I think we will have some hard times this summer," a soldier named T. P. Eagan wrote to his sister. "The old chief Sitting Bull says that he will not make peace with the whites as long as he has a man to fight."

Custer's Not Worried

T. P. Eagan and the rest of George Armstrong Custer's Seventh Cavalry rode away from Fort Abraham Lincoln, off to find Sitting Bull and drive him onto a reservation. Everyone knew it would be a risky job. "The wives and children of the soldiers lined the road," Elizabeth Custer remembered. "Mothers, with streaming eyes, held their little ones out at arm's length for one last look at the departing father."

Then the soldiers marched away. All the families could do was stay in the fort and wait for news.

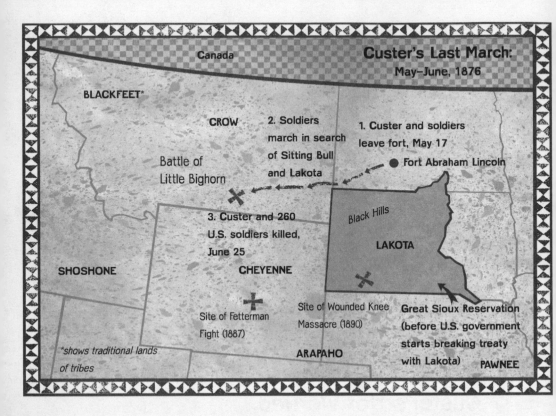

Custer's Last March:
May–June, 1876

Canada

BLACKFEET*

CROW

2. Soldiers march in search of Sitting Bull and Lakota

1. Custer and soldiers leave fort, May 17

● Fort Abraham Lincoln

Battle of Little Bighorn

Black Hills

3. Custer and 260 U.S. soldiers killed, June 25

LAKOTA

SHOSHONE

CHEYENNE

Site of Fetterman Fight (1887)

Site of Wounded Knee Massacre (1890)

Great Sioux Reservation (before U.S. government starts breaking treaty with Lakota)

*shows traditional lands of tribes

ARAPAHO

PAWNEE

"We have not seen any signs of Indians thus far," Custer wrote to his wife on May 20. He added that he and his brother, an officer in his unit, were having a wonderful time. "Tom and I have fried onions at breakfast and dinner," he wrote, "and raw onions for lunch!"

"They both took advantage of their first absence from home to partake of their favorite vegetable," Elizabeth noted. "Onions were permitted at our table, but after indulging in them they found themselves severely let alone, and that they did not enjoy."

Custer sent an update on June 21: his scouts had found a fresh trail left by a large group of Indians. "I feel hopeful of accomplishing great results," he wrote.

"I have but a few moments to write," he added the next day. "We move at twelve, and I have my hands full of preparations. . . . Do not be anxious about me. . . . I hope to have a good report to send you by the next mail."

Two days later Custer stood on a hilltop looking through binoculars toward a huge Indian camp along the banks of the winding Little Bighorn River.

"The largest Indian camp on the North American continent is ahead and I am going to attack it."

George Armstrong Custer

Determined to surprise his enemy, Custer decided to attack without taking time to study the geography or find out how many warriors he might be facing. He divided his forces, leading 210 men toward the camp himself. Another force, led by Major Marcus Reno, approached the camp from a different direction.

"We'll find enough Sioux to keep us fighting two or three days," predicted a Crow Indian who was working as a scout for Custer.

Custer shook his head. "I guess we'll get through them in one day," he said.

181

Strong Hearts to the Front!

"It was somewhere past the middle of the afternoon, and all of us were having a good time," remembered a Cheyenne woman of the moment before Custer's attack on June 25, 1876.

More than six thousand Lakota, Cheyenne, and other Indian allies—including about two thousand warriors—were camped along the Little Bighorn. They knew the Americans were out there somewhere. "I was thirteen years old and not very big for my age," remembered Black Elk, "but I thought I should have to be a man anyway." He was swimming with friends in the Little Bighorn when he heard sudden shouts:

"The chargers are coming!"

"They are charging!"

Black Elk ran to his family's lodge for his rifle. His friend Iron Hawk, who was fourteen, also prepared for battle. "I was so shaky that it took me a long time to braid an eagle feather into my hair," he said.

Nearby, young warriors ran into Sitting Bull's lodge, shouting that Custer was attacking. "I jumped up and stepped out," said Sitting Bull. He saw waves of blue-coated American soldiers blasting away as they charged on horses into camp. "The bullets were like humming bees," he said. "We thought we were whipped."

"They came on us like a thunderbolt," said a Lakota chief named Low Dog. "I never before nor since saw men so brave and fearless as those white warriors."

Crazy Horse helped rally the Indian forces, shouting: "It is a good day to fight! It is a good day to die! Strong hearts, brave hearts, to the front! Weak hearts and cowards to the rear!"

"Then came the rush of the enemy," said Billy Jackson, an American soldier who was part of Major Reno's charge. Jackson and the other soldiers suddenly saw at least five hundred Indian warriors charging toward them. "Their shots, their war cries, the thunder of their horses' feet were deafening," Jackson said.

Somewhere in the middle of this chaos, Custer was waving his hat and shouting, "Courage, boys, we've got them!" But now that Custer was in the Indian camp, he must have realized how badly outnumbered his soldiers were. It was too late to do anything but try to fight his way out.

Witnesses described the next few minutes as a confusing mix of swirling dust, gunshots, and shouts of pain and fury. Custer's soldiers split into smaller groups, but they were all quickly surrounded. "I think they were so scared that they didn't know what they were doing," Black Elk said. "The shooting was quick, quick, pop—pop—

pop, very fast," said a warrior named Two Moons. "We circled all around them—swirling like water round a stone."

With no time to reload, men swung their guns at each other like clubs. They wrestled and punched and bit. Many of Custer's soldiers finally threw down their weapons. They were ready to surrender.

But the Indians kept on attacking. Sitting Bull's cousin watched Indian warriors shooting and stabbing Custer's men after they tried to surrender. "The blood of the people was hot and their hearts bad," she said, "and they took no prisoners that day."

Death All Around

Major Reno and his surviving soldiers—who had attacked from the other side of the Indian camp—never saw what happened to Custer. They spent an endless night on a nearby hill, wondering why they received no messages or orders from Custer. "We felt terribly alone on that dangerous hilltop," said a soldier named Charles Windolph. "We were a million miles from nowhere. And death was all around us."

When Reno's men finally made it to safety, they found out why they hadn't heard from Custer. "We had a closer view of Custer's battlefield," one of the soldiers said. "We saw a large number of objects that looked like white boulders scattered over the field."

As they walked nearer, they realized that these were not boulders. They were the bodies of Custer's soldiers, stripped and badly cut up. The men wept as they walked among the bodies, looking for friends.

Meanwhile, back at Fort Abraham Lincoln, the soldiers' families were suffering through the hot summer of 1876, waiting for news. "Our little group of saddened women, borne down with one common weight of anxiety, sought solace in gathering together in our house," said Elizabeth Custer.

One day, while the women were singing to pass the time, a messenger arrived. It was an Indian named Horn Toad, one of Custer's scouts. Panting from exhaustion, he delivered the news in short sentences: "Custer killed. Whole command killed."

Horn Toad's report was accurate. Custer and every one of the 210 men he led into battle were dead. Another fifty men from Major Reno's force had been killed. It was by far the biggest defeat the American military ever suffered in the Indian wars.

The news from Little Bighorn shocked the entire nation— coming right at the moment Americans were celebrating the country's one hundredth birthday. General William T. Sherman promised to send more soldiers west to crush the Lakota once and for all.

After Little Bighorn

Back at Little Bighorn, Sitting Bull and the other chiefs realized they had won a historic victory. They also knew Sherman. They knew he would come after them harder than ever now, and they were not really prepared. The recent fighting had left them nearly out of ammunition.

The huge Indian camp on the Little Bighorn split up, with smaller groups marching off in different directions.

Sherman's forces went on the attack right away, just as the harsh northern plains winter began. "The worse it gets, the better," said General George Crook, who led the attacks. "Always hunt Indians in bad weather."

Crook pushed his shivering soldiers on long marches across the frozen plains. "I know it looks hard, but we've got to do it, and it shall be done," he said. "If necessary we can eat our horses."

"I'd as soon think of eating my brother," grumbled a young officer (not loud enough for the general to hear).

All winter Crook's soldiers surprised Lakota and Cheyenne villages, capturing horses and destroying food supplies. Indians who survived the attacks were scattered in the snow without food or tents. After attacking one village, an American soldier reported: "The thermometer never got higher than 25 below. . . . Those poor Cheyenne were out there in that weather with nothing to eat, no shelter."

Sitting Bull led about one thousand people across the border into Canada, where they were safe from American attacks. But for those unable to escape, there was little chance of finding food on the plains. Buffalo were getting scarce now. As the winter dragged on, groups of Indians started coming in to reservations. "I am tired of being always on the watch for troops," explained Red Horse, a Lakota chief. "My desire is to get my family where they can sleep without being continually in the expectation of an attack."

The Lakota teenager Black Elk felt the same way. "Wherever we went, the soldiers came to kill us," he said of that winter. He and his family went in to a reservation. There, in May 1877, he watched the surrender of a leader he had grown up idolizing. "Crazy Horse came in with the rest of our people," said Black Elk, "and the ponies that were only skin and bones."

American soldiers took the famous warrior's weapons. They handed him some beef and beans.

"I want this peace to last forever," Crazy Horse said.

General Crook wanted peace too. But he had his own ideas about how to keep it— he wanted Crazy Horse locked up.

Crazy Horse

A group of soldiers surrounded Crazy Horse. They reached for his arms.

"Don't touch me!" he yelled.

The soldiers started dragging him across the reservation. When he saw he was being taken toward a tiny jail cell, Crazy Horse yanked free and pulled out a knife.

"Kill him! Kill him!" soldiers shouted.

A soldier lunged forward and stabbed Crazy Horse with his bayonet. A few other soldiers reached for the fallen warrior.

"Let me go, my friends," Crazy Horse said. "You have got me hurt enough." Crazy Horse died that night. "I cried all night, and so did my father," Black Elk said.

Chief Joseph's Promise

From his homeland in Oregon, Chief Joseph of the Nez Perce watched the fall of the powerful Plains Indians. The message was clear: Indians could win battles against American soldiers. But even the most powerful groups could not win wars against the United States.

Joseph was determined to help the Nez Perce hold on to their traditional territory in Oregon's Wallowa Valley. He had sworn to his dying father that he would never give up this land.

"You must stop your ears whenever you are asked to sign a treaty selling your home," Joseph's father told him. "My son, never forget my dying words. This country holds your father's body. Never sell the bones of your father and mother."

"I pressed my father's hand and told him I would protect his grave with my life," Joseph said.

This promise put Joseph in an impossible position in 1877. Actually, it wasn't the promise that caused trouble—it was that American settlers were moving onto Nez Perce land.

How was Joseph supposed to defend this land once the United States decided to take it?

The End of the Wild West

In April 1877, General Oliver O. Howard left his headquarters in Portland, Oregon, and headed east. He had new orders: Clear the Nez Perce off their land and move them to a reservation in Idaho. Privately, Howard sympathized with the Indians, telling friends: "It is a great mistake to take from Joseph and his band of Nez Perce Indians that valley." But Howard had his orders. He continued toward the Wallowa Valley to deliver the government's demand.

You've Heard This One

It was the same old story. Gold had been found on the Nez Perce land, and settlers raced in. They started putting up cabins, fencing in farms, stealing Nez Perce cattle. Both sides were ready to fight for the land. Hoping to avoid another costly Indian war, the government offered the Nez Perce land on a reservation in nearby Idaho. It wasn't really an offer.

The Nez Perce realized this when General Oliver Howard showed up in May 1877. Howard told them to pack up and leave the Wallowa Valley. If they didn't get moving, Howard warned, the army would come and give them a shove.

Joseph and the other chiefs told Howard they had never agreed to be moved from their homeland. "Chief Toohoolhoolzote stood up to talk for the Indians," remembered a young Nez Perce named Yellow Wolf. "He told how the land always belonged to the Indians." This led to an angry argument with Howard:

Howard: *You know very well that the government has set apart a reservation, and that the Indians must go on it.*

Toohoolhoolzote: *Who are you to tell me what to do? What person pretends to divide the land?*

Howard: *I am that man. I stand here for the president. My orders are plain and will be executed.*

Toohoolhoolzote: *We came from the earth, and our bodies must go back to the earth, our mother.*

Howard: *I don't want to offend your religion, but you must talk about practicable things. Twenty times over I hear that the earth is your mother. . . . I want to hear no more, but come to business at once.*

Toohoolhoolzote: *Who can tell me what I must do in my own country? Are you the Great Spirit? Did you make the world? Did you make the sun?*

Howard finally got sick of arguing. He told the Nez Perce they had thirty days to leave their land.

"Why are you in such a hurry?" Joseph asked. "I cannot get ready to move in thirty days." He explained that they would need more time to gather their animals and collect supplies for the coming winter.

"If you let the time run over one day," Howard warned, "the soldiers will be there to drive you onto the reservation."

Howard's threat sparked a fierce debate among the Nez Perce. "I did not want bloodshed," Joseph said. "I did not want my people killed. I did not want anybody killed." He argued that it would be better to move than to see their people killed in a war that could never be won.

But many of the younger chiefs and warriors vowed to stay and fight. "Toohoolhoolzote talked for war," Joseph remembered, "and made many of my young men

willing to fight rather than be driven like dogs from the land where they were born."

While Joseph made preparations to leave, a group of young warriors left the village at night, marched to nearby cabins, and killed four settlers. "I would have given my own life if I could have undone the killing of white men by my people," Joseph said.

Now, he knew, General Howard would be sending his soldiers to fight the Nez Perce. Now there was no way to avoid war.

The Flight of the Nez Perce

"I t was just like two bulldogs meeting," Yellow Wolf said of the moment he and other Nez Perce warriors slammed into the American soldiers. "We drove them back across the mountain, down to near the town they came from."

Thirty-three Americans were killed in this quick battle. "I never went up against anything like the Nez Perces in all my life," said one of the surviving soldiers.

The young Nez Perce warriors celebrated. But Joseph and the other chiefs knew Howard would be back soon, and with a much bigger army. With only about 150 warriors, the Nez Perce could not simply wait here to be attacked. Their only choice was to start moving.

"From that time, the Nez Perce had no more rest," Yellow Wolf remembered.

About seven hundred Nez Perce men, women, and children quickly packed everything they and their animals could carry. Then they headed east toward the open spaces of Montana. There they hoped to meet up with the Crow Indians, old allies of theirs.

When he saw the Nez Perce moving, General Howard and his

five hundred soldiers set off to catch them. They chased the Nez Perce out of Oregon and into the rugged Bitterroot Mountains of Idaho. As news of the chase spread, people in nearby towns panicked and locked themselves in their cabins (parents in one town locked their children in the vault of the local bank).

In western Montana a small group of soldiers gathered to try to block the path of the oncoming Nez Perce. After laying logs across the road, the men declared: "You cannot get by us."

"We are going by you without fighting if you will let us," Joseph answered. "But we are going by you, anyhow."

Suddenly feeling extremely outnumbered, the soldiers got out of the way. And the chase continued across Montana, then south back into Idaho, and east into Wyoming. "We rode on, always watching for enemies," Yellow Wolf said. As one of the Nez Perce scouts, he had the vital job of watching for Howard's army. Only during rare moments of rest did he allow himself to think about home:

"Thoughts came of the Wallowa where I grew up. Of my own country when only Indians were there. Of tepees along the bending river. Of the blue, clear lake, wide meadows with horse and cattle herds."

Yellow Wolf

Where was General Howard's army meanwhile? That's what the entire country was wondering. By now Americans everywhere were following the amazing chase in their newspapers. An increasingly irritated General Sherman sent Howard telegrams with orders such as: "That force of yours should pursue the Nez Perce to the death."

Race to the Border

As Howard pushed his men harder, exhausted soldiers wore through their boots and had to tie rags around their bloody feet. They shivered through rainy nights, unable to start fires with only wet buffalo chips for fuel. And all they had to eat was rotting pork and biscuits so hard that they had to be soaked overnight before they were soft enough to chew.

The Nez Perce were running out of food too. Some of the older men and women were getting too weak and tired to continue. When they couldn't take another step, they asked to be wrapped in blankets and set in the shade. Everyone knew they would die there.

By late August the Nez Perce finally met up with their Crow allies in Montana. It was a disappointing reunion. The Crows explained that they had seen what had just happened to the Lakota and Cheyenne after Little Bighorn. They were not willing to take sides against the United States.

All alone now, and far from home, the Nez Perce had one last chance—they could make a run for Canada. If they could get across the border, they might be able to team up with Sitting Bull and the Lakota who had followed him north.

The Nez Perce hurried in that direction, reaching the Bear Paw Mountains in late September. After traveling more than 1,700 miles in three months, they were just two days from the Canadian border. "We knew General Howard was more than two suns back on our trail," Yellow Wolf said. In fact, warriors started calling Howard "General Day-and-a-Half-Behind."

What they didn't know was that another American army, commanded by Colonel Nelson Miles, was racing toward their camp from the east. As Joseph and the Nez Perce rested for their final march to Canada, Miles and his army were less than fifteen miles away.

Fight No More

The Nez Perce were packing up for their last march north when scouts came galloping into camp, shouting:

"Soldiers! Soldiers!"

"Enemies right on us!"

Moments later Colonel Miles and his six hundred soldiers charged into camp.

"My little daughter, twelve years old, was with me," Joseph remembered. "I gave her a rope, and told her to catch a horse."

Joseph's daughter and many others were able to get away while Joseph and the warriors tried to fight off the attack. "Six of my men were killed in one spot near me," Joseph said. "I called my men to drive them back. We fought at close range, not more than twenty steps apart."

Many of the best Nez Perce warriors died in a bloody, daylong battle. Miles had the camp surrounded by nightfall. The next morning, as snow started falling, he began blasting shells into camp. The Nez Perce dug holes in the snow for protection from the bombs and the cold. But they were nearly out of food.

After five days of this, Colonel Miles demanded surrender. "If you will come out and give up your arms," he said, "I will spare your lives and send you to your reservation."

Some of the surviving chiefs wanted to fight on to the death. But Joseph was desperate to save as many lives as he could. "I am tired of fighting," he told the Americans.

"It is cold and we have no blankets. The little children are freezing to death. My people, some of them, have run away to the hills, and have no blankets, no food; no one knows where they are—perhaps freezing to death. I want to have time to look for my children and see how many of them I can find. Maybe I shall find them among the dead. Hear me, my chiefs! I am tired; my heart is sick and sad. From where the sun now stands I will fight no more forever."

Chief Joseph

Joseph demanded that the Nez Perce be allowed to travel in safety to the reservation in Idaho. Miles agreed. The men shook hands.

Then Sherman heard about the deal—and threw another fit. "The Indians are prisoners, and their wishes should not be consulted," he told Miles.

Sherman wanted to send a chilling signal to any other Indian groups that might be thinking about standing up to the United States. He ordered the Nez Perce taken on another long journey, one thousand miles east and south by riverboat and train. Joseph and the Nez Perce were dumped off on a hot and buggy piece of reservation land in Indian Territory—today's Oklahoma.

The government told them: *Now you can learn to live like civilized people.*

Exodusters Head West

While all this was happening, the massive movement of Americans from east to west was still going strong—thanks, in part, to Benjamin Singleton.

Singleton had escaped from slavery before the Civil War. Returning to the South after the war, he saw that former slaves had no real chance of improving their lives. White landowners simply refused to sell any land to black families.

Singleton came up with a plan. He started a settlement in Kansas, where land was still available to homesteaders. Then he printed posters and advertisements, sending them all over the South, inspiring thousands of African Americans to move west. They called themselves Exodusters (because they saw similarities between their story and the biblical book of Exodus, in which the Israelite people escape from slavery).

Members of Congress started wondering why so many African American families were suddenly heading west. They called on Benjamin Singleton to testify before a Senate committee in 1880. Singleton told the senators he'd been leading black settlers to Kansas for seven years. "I believe I fetched out 7,432 people," he said.

Senator: *How did you happen to send them out?*

Singleton: *The first cause, do you mean, of them going?*

Senator: *Yes.*

Singleton: *Well, my people, for the want of land—we needed land for our children—and their disadvantages—that caused my heart to grieve and sorrow; pity for my race, sir . . . that caused me to go to work for them.*

Senator: *You take all that responsibility on yourself?*

Benjamin Singleton

200

Singleton: *I do . . . and I think I have done a good deal of good, and I feel relieved!*

Senator: *You are proud of your work?*

Singleton: *Yes, sir; I am!*

Historians aren't sure Singleton got the number (7,432) exactly right. But we do know he was a key leader of the Exoduster movement. And we know that thousands of Exodusters set out in search of new opportunities in the West.

Of course, they faced all the same challenges as other pioneers— greater challenges, really, because as slaves they had never had the chance to save up any money. But like other pioneers, they were determined to start new lives on their own land. When one newspaper reporter asked an African American woman if the hardships might drive her back to the South, she said, "What, go back! Oh, no; I'd sooner starve here."

An Exoduster named Williana Hickman had a slightly different reaction when her wagon first rattled into Kansas. She heard her husband and men in nearby wagons shouting: "There is Nicodemus!"

Battered and exhausted from the journey, Hickman was relieved to finally be arriving at Nicodemus, a town founded recently by black pioneers. She looked out from the wagon. There was nothing in sight but flat, open grassland.

"Where is Nicodemus?" she asked. "I don't see it."

Her husband pointed ahead to a few snake-like curls of smoke rising from holes in the ground. "That is Nicodemus," he said.

And she realized what he meant. Everyone in town was living underground in dugouts. "The scenery was not at all inviting," she said.

The scenery changed quickly, though. Ten years later Nicodemus was a thriving town, with newspapers, hotels, churches, stores (including an ice cream shop), and a baseball team.

Towns Everywhere

Towns were popping up all over the Great Plains those days. Maybe the strangest of them was Runnymede, Kansas, founded by an immigrant from Britain named Ned Turnly. Actually, it wasn't so much a town as a get-rich-quick scheme.

Turnly traveled around Britain, meeting with rich parents and offering to take their sons to America to teach them how to farm—for a fee of five hundred pounds. Lots of families liked the idea of sending their spoiled young men off to learn about real work.

Of course, the sons had no interest in busting their backs on the plains of Kansas. So Turnly took them aside and said: *Never mind the farming. Come to America with me and you can hunt and play sports all day.* The young men were eager to sign up.

About a hundred of them arrived in Runnymede with their rifles, their favorite hunting dogs, and lots of spending money. They quickly set up horseracing tracks, a polo field, tennis courts, and fox hunts (though they usually hunted jackrabbits, which were easier to find).

While other pioneers were battling grasshoppers and droughts and prairie fires, these men faced dangers of their own, as one local newspaper reported: "Mr. Horace Capel had a rather nasty accident in the bowling alley the other evening—he got his thumb jammed between one of the pins and a ball." Poor Horace lost his fingernail and needed a few stitches. "From the latest reports we hear he is progressing favorably," the paper assured readers.

It was even riskier to join the town's football club (soccer, as we call it). Curious to see this imported sport, a reporter from a nearby town came to a game at Runnymede. He watched men run around kicking a ball, though to him the whole thing looked like an enormous wrestling match. "It was startling to witness them throw one another around violently," he reported. "How many of them escaped serious injury is a mystery to the writer."

The fun didn't last, though. Runnymede's whole economy was based on money from families back in Britain—and when the families heard what their boys were up to in America, they stopped sending money. That was the end of Runnymede.

But other towns all over the West (places with less bowling, more working) continued to grow. Nat Love saw the whole thing happen from the saddle of his horse. Still working as a cowboy, still riding the long cattle drives, Love watched the wide-open spaces of the West fill up with settlers. "The immense cattle ranges, stretching away in the distance as far as the eye could see, now began to be dotted with cities and towns," Love said.

"To us wild cowboys of the range," he added, "the new order of things did not appeal."

The Last to Surrender

Sitting Bull would probably have agreed.

The Lakota chief had spent several years in Canada, but food was always hard to find. Besides, he wanted to go home. In the summer of 1881, riding bony horses and wearing ragged clothes, Sitting Bull and about forty families crossed the border to the United States.

All the Plains Indians were living on reservations now. Sitting Bull knew that he too must go to a reservation and turn himself in. For a man of tremendous pride, this was the toughest act of his life. In fact, he couldn't bring himself to hand over his rifle to American soldiers. Instead, he had his son Crow Foot (five years old) hand over the weapon.

"I surrender this rifle to you through my young son, whom I now desire to teach in this manner that he has become a friend of the Americans. . . . I wish it to be remembered that I was the last man of my tribe to surrender my rifle."

Then he tried to settle into life on the reservation. This wasn't easy, since the government kept coming up with new plans to carve off pieces of Indian reservations and open the land to settlers. After being forced to move five times by the government, one chief joked bitterly: "I think you had better put the Indians on wheels, and you can run them about whenever you wish."

At shrinking reservations all over the West, government agents tried to persuade Indians to plant crops and raise cattle. The Americans put Sitting Bull to work digging a garden, which he found incredibly boring. He expressed his feelings in a song:

A warrior I have been
Now it is all over
A hard time I have

Finally Sitting Bull got permission to travel around a bit by train (he couldn't leave the reservation without a government pass). He saw some towns, toured some factories, made some speeches. And he was somewhat surprised to see huge crowds following him everywhere—he hadn't realized he was one of the most famous people in America. Fame didn't really impress Sitting Bull, though he liked when people paid him to sign autographs.

Then life in the new America got even weirder for Sitting Bull. In 1885 a showman (and former buffalo hunter) named William "Buffalo Bill" Cody invited the Lakota chief to join Buffalo Bill's Wild West Show. The show claimed to give audiences in eastern cities a look at what life used to be like in the West. Sitting Bull's role in the show was to set up a tepee and ride around on a horse in his traditional clothing.

The show traveled from city to city, playing to sold-out theaters. Sitting Bull was making a great salary, plus extras from selling autographs and photos. He never got rich, though. He handed out most of his money to poor children he met on the streets of American cities.

After a year of touring, Sitting Bull got sick of show business. He went back home to the Plains—back to the boring life on the Standing Rock Indian Reservation.

The Weather's Still Wild

No, the West just wasn't as exciting as it used to be. Unless you count the weather.

Take January 12, 1888, for example. The sun was shining at noon, and it was unusually warm. A schoolboy named O. W. Coursey was having fun with his friends outside their Dakota schoolhouse.

"We were all out playing in our shirt sleeves," said Coursey, "without hats or mittens. Suddenly we looked up and saw something coming rolling toward us with great fury from the northwest, and making a loud noise."

It looked to Corsey like mountains of cotton tumbling through the air, heading right for them. The children dove into the schoolhouse just as the blizzard slammed into the building, nearly knocking it over.

This massive storm of snow and wind swept across the plains, sending temperatures diving to twenty below zero. So many kids were at school when the storm hit that it became known as the School Children's Blizzard. Suddenly stuck in dark, freezing schoolhouses, many students tried to run for home—a very bad idea. The swirling snow turned the entire world white. Kids got hopelessly lost just a few feet from the building.

A nineteen-year-old teacher named Minnie Freeman didn't have the option of staying inside. When the blizzard hit her Nebraska schoolhouse it ripped off the door and sent the roof spinning into the sky. Freeman knew her seventeen students could not live long without shelter. She quickly tied them together with a long piece of string, then led them out into the icy wind. "How it cut and almost blinded them!" she said. "It was terrible on their eyes."

They stumbled and felt their way forward for nearly a mile. Amazingly, though she couldn't see more than a foot in front of her, Freeman was able to find a nearby farmhouse. She became a national celebrity for her heroism that day. (She got eighty marriage proposals in the mail.) Others were not so lucky. More than two hundred people died in the storm, many of them children who got lost trying to get home.

As settlers on the Great Plains were learning, these kinds of blizzards could strike at any time during the long winter. This changed life in the West, because ranchers got sick of losing their animals in storms. The cattle would wander off and their hooves would get frozen to the ground. Unable to move, they would freeze or starve to death before the ranchers could find them.

To protect their herds, ranchers started fencing in their land with a new invention: barbed wire. Farmers were doing the same thing. And the West was gradually divided up into fenced-in farms and ranches.

Rush for the Last Land

Was there any good farmland still available in the West? Yes, but it was in the huge chunk of land called Indian Territory, where more than fifty tribes were living. Congress studied the maps—and decided Indians didn't need quite so much land. The government bought big pieces of the territory and declared the land would soon be open to settlers.

That explains what 100,000 people were doing on the border of Indian Territory on the warm, sunny morning of April 22, 1889. The government had announced that two million acres would be open to settlers at noon. What did you have to do to claim 160 acres? Just be the first one there.

When the army bugler began blowing at noon, his horn was instantly drowned out by the thundering clomp of feet pounding dirt. People raced ahead on horses, on foot, on bicycles.

A reporter named William Howard joined the land rush just to watch the action. "A cloud of dust rose where the home-seekers had stood in line," he wrote, "and when it had drifted away before the gentle breeze, the horses and wagons and men were tearing across the open country like fiends." Of course, people on fast horses pulled into the lead. They hurried to the land they wanted—only to find other homesteaders had gotten there sooner. It was pretty obvious these "sooners" had snuck onto the land before it was legally open for settlement. One guy was even found sitting on a claim where the leafy tops of vegetables could clearly be seen sprouting from a garden! (He said he had planted the seeds fifteen minutes before. *The soil must be very fertile,* he explained.)

Before the sun set that evening, settlers had claimed all two million acres. They even built cities overnight. Cities of tents, at least. The next morning the population of Oklahoma City was 10,000 (up from zero the day before). "Never before in the history of the West has so large a number of people been concentrated in one place in so short a time," reported William Howard.

The government opened other sections of nearby land over the next few years, setting off new land rushes. The Indian Territory soon became the state of Oklahoma.

Dancing in the Snow

The West was clearly changing forever. In 1890 thousands of Indians made a last, desperate attempt to hold on to their old traditions.

"Suddenly great excitement came into our midst," remembered Luther Standing Bear. The son of a Lakota chief, he was now teaching English to Lakota children at the Rosebud Reservation in South Dakota. "It broke so suddenly that a great many of the Indians did not know which way to turn," he said. "It was the craze of a new religion called the 'Ghost Dance.'"

The Ghost Dance movement was founded by a Paiute Indian in Nevada named Wovoka. By performing this new dance, Wovoka taught, Indians could peacefully bring back their traditional way of life. Buffalo herds would return. White settlers would disappear. Indians would live on a new earth.

"When I first heard of it, I thought it was only foolish talk," said Black Elk, who was then in his late twenties. "I thought it was only the despair that made people believe."

Whatever the reason, many did believe. Indians began dancing on reservations from North Dakota all the way to Arizona. By November 1890 the Ghost Dance had taken over life on many reservations—people stopped working on farms or going to school.

Government agents running the reservations were getting nervous. "Indians are dancing in the snow and are wild and crazy," complained an agent at the Pine Ridge Reservation in South Dakota. "We need protection and we need it now."

Agents at the Standing Rock Reservation blamed Sitting Bull, claiming he was secretly behind this movement (he wasn't). They wanted him to tell everyone to stop dancing.

Sitting Bull refused. He wasn't sure he believed in the dance himself, but he saw no reason to stop others from following whatever religion they chose.

Fearing a huge Indian rebellion, the army started sending soldiers to reservations. At Standing Rock a group of Indians working as policemen were told to arrest Sitting Bull.

"What do you want here?" he asked when the policemen came to take him away.

"You are my prisoner," said one of the men.

"All right," Sitting Bull sighed. "Let me put on my clothes and I'll go with you."

But as the police led Sitting Bull outside, his supporters rushed forward and crowded around.

"You think you are going to take him!" shouted an Indian named Catch-the-Bear. "You shall not do it!" Then to the gathering crowd he called: "Come on now, let us protect our chief!"

Angry people rushed forward, pushing, waving fists, shouting. Catch-the-Bear raised his rifle and shot a policeman. Several policemen fired their own guns into the crowd.

Sitting Bull was hit twice. He fell dead to the ground.

A Dream Dies at Wounded Knee

Now fearing for their own safety, about four hundred Indians fled from Standing Rock Reservation. They spent the night of December 28, 1890, camped along the banks of Wounded Knee Creek.

Early the next morning a Lakota man named Dewey Beard heard

an army bugle slice through the cold air. "I saw the soldiers mounting their horses and surrounding us," he remembered. "It was announced that all men should come to the center for a talk."

About five hundred American soldiers had the Lakota surrounded, with big guns pointing into camp from all directions. The soldiers demanded that the Lakota give up their weapons. Most quickly gave up the guns. While searching for more weapons, soldiers found a rifle hidden under a blanket worn by a young man named Black Coyote.

Black Coyote wriggled free and pulled out his rifle and held it above his head.

Soldiers yelled at him to drop the gun. They had no way of knowing he was deaf.

"If they had left him alone he was going to put his gun down," Dewey Beard later said. But soldiers charged Black Coyote. He shot into the air as they grabbed him.

Then there was a huge explosion of gunfire from the soldiers. Lakota warriors tried to fight back, but they had given up most of their weapons.

"We tried to run," remembered one Lakota woman, "but they shot us like we were buffalo." In less than an hour of fighting, more than 150 Lakota men, women, and children were killed.

Walking through the Wounded Knee camp that night, an American soldier counted the bodies frozen to the icy ground. "It was a thing to melt the heart of a man, if it was of stone," he said. Black Elk also saw the twisted bodies lying in bunches. He was haunted by the sight for the rest of his life.

"And I can see that something else died there in the bloody mud, and was buried there in the blizzard. A people's dream died there. It was a beautiful dream."

Wounded Knee was the last major fight between American soldiers and Native Americans. All the Indian groups of the American West had now been driven onto reservations. The Indian population of the United States stood at 237,000—the lowest total since the arrival of European settlers. (The Native American population of the United States today is about 2.5 million.)

Black Elk

The Cowboys Retire

In contrast, the population of the United States zoomed toward 70 million. And more than 17 million Americans were now living west of the Mississippi River.

The United States government now declared that the West was officially "settled." Before, there had always been a frontier in the West—a line separating settled land from unsettled land. But in 1892 the government reported: "There can hardly be said to be a frontier line."

How do you know the West had really changed forever? Simple: the cowboys started retiring.

"From now on I wasn't a cowpuncher anymore," said Teddy "Blue" Abbott. The huge open plains the cowboys had used for cattle drives were gone, divided into farms and ranches and towns. And there was no need to drive cattle north now anyway. New railroads ran through Texas and the other southern states, so trains could pick up the cows right there.

Teddy Abbott settled in Montana and found work as a guard at a gold mine. He saved up money, married his sweetheart,

Mary, and then did something truly shocking: he became a farmer! "I took a homestead," he said, "kept milk cows and raised a garden."

Nat Love's story was similar. "With the march of progress came the railroad and no longer were we called upon to follow the long-horned steers," he said. Love tried working at a big fenced-in ranch, but it just wasn't the same. "I bid farewell to the life which I had followed for over twenty years," he said. "It was with genuine regret that I left the longhorn Texas cattle and the wild mustangs of the range, but the life had in a great measure lost its attractions and so I decided to quit it and try something else for a while."

With a new century ahead, Love turned to his attention to new adventures and new challenges. So did the rest of the country.

What Ever Happened to . . . ?

 "I had always worked for big cow outfits and looked down on settlers," remembered the cowboy-turned-farmer **Teddy "Blue" Abbott**. "Now I was on the other side of the fence, and finding out how damn hard it was to start out poor and get anywheres." With years of hard work, Teddy and his wife, Mary, did get somewhere—they built a two-thousand-acre farm and ranch, and raised eight children. He always enjoyed meeting up with old cowboys and swapping stories about life on the trail. "Only a few of us left now," he said in 1938, when he was seventy-eight years old. "The rest have left the wagon and gone ahead across the big divide." Abbott crossed the divide himself a year later.

 When the newly independent Republic of Texas held its first presidential election in 1836, **Stephen F. Austin** was pretty sure he'd get the gig. "The prosperity of Texas has been the object of my labors," Austin said. "It has assumed the character of a religion, for the guidance of my thoughts and actions, for fifteen years." But then, two weeks before the vote, the war hero Sam Houston jumped into the contest—and clobbered Austin (5,119 to 587). Later that year Austin developed pneumonia and died at the age of forty-three. Over time, Texans started to appreciate him more—they even named their capital city for him.

After spending eight years as a Crow chief, the African American mountain man **James Beckwourth** turned to other adventures: army scout, wagon driver, trader, hotel owner, guide, gambler, gold miner. He slowed down just long enough to dictate his autobiography, *The Life and Adventures of James P. Beckwourth,* a big hit when it came out in 1856. (Beckwourth was supposed to get half the profits; he never got a dime.) The book is still famous for its priceless descriptions of real life in the Wild West. Beckwourth eventually returned to Crow territory, where he died in 1866, at the age of sixty-eight.

 After the defeat of the Lakota, **Black Elk** remained a highly respected healer and holy man. Like Sitting Bull, he was offered a job with a traveling Wild West show. "My relatives told me I should stay at home and go on curing people," he remembered. But he wanted to see a bit of the world. The show took him across the ocean to London, where he performed for Queen Victoria. ("She was little but fat and we liked her," he recalled.) In 1931, when he was an old man and nearly blind, he told his life story in a book called *Black Elk Speaks*—an all-time classic account of the traditional life and religious beliefs of his people.

 Upon returning from the Lewis and Clark Expedition, **William Clark** settled in St. Louis, ran a successful fur company, got married, and had five kids. While serving as territorial governor of Missouri, Clark was accused by some of being too friendly to Indians. He responded with an opinion that would be largely ignored in the decades to come (forgive his spelling and grammar): "It is to be lamented that this deplorable situation of the Indians do not receive more of the humain feelings of this nation." When Missouri joined the Union in 1820, Clark ran for governor. He lost. He kept busy, though, constantly updating his beloved maps of the West until his death in 1838.

 After working for a while at a Nevada newspaper, **Samuel Clemens** realized he had a talent for writing funny stories. "It is nothing to be proud of," he told his brother, "but it is my strongest suit." Calling himself Mark Twain, he settled far from the Wild West (Connecticut) and wrote some of the most famous books in American literature (*The Adventures of Tom Sawyer, Adventures of Huckleberry Finn,* and many more). His humor turned bitter as he aged, as you can tell from one of his later jokes: "Reader, suppose you were an idiot. And suppose you were a member of Congress. But I repeat myself." When a story spread in 1897 that Twain was on his deathbed, he responded with a classic line: "The reports of my death are greatly exaggerated." He died for real in 1910, at the age of seventy-five.

 Henry "Old Pancake" Comstock and his partners may have discovered a $400 million gold and silver mine, but as usual with major strikes, the real money was made by wealthy investors. Comstock sold his share of the mine for $11,000, invested the money in a store, lost everything, and shot himself. His partners fared no better. One got drunk, fell off his horse, and died of a cracked skull. The other began hearing voices, was sent to a hospital for the insane, and died there. Careful what you wish for.

After George Armstrong Custer's death at Little Bighorn, **Elizabeth Custer** packed up, traveled back east—and found out the whole country was arguing about her husband. Some called Custer a fearless hero who died defending his country. Others said he was a reckless glory-seeker whose thirst for fame had led to disaster. What really stunned Elizabeth was President Ulysses S. Grant's opinion: "I regard Custer's massacre as a sacrifice of troops brought on by Custer himself." Elizabeth Custer spent the rest of her life (and she lived another fifty-seven years) trying to rescue her husband's reputation. It worked. "General Custer's name was a shining light to all the youth of America," remembered Theodore Roosevelt, a teenager at the time of Little Bighorn. In more recent years (without his wife around to defend him) historians have been much tougher on Custer.

As a lead builder of the transcontinental railroad, **Thomas Durant** had bragged that he would "grab a wad of money from the construction fees—and get out." And that's exactly what he did. He "got out" just in time too, leaving the Union Pacific shortly before the *New York Sun* ran the huge headline "THE KING OF FRAUDS—COLOSSAL BRIBERY." The story exposed the fact that Durant and friends had handed out cash and stock to members of Congress in exchange for laws helping the railroad. Durant shrugged and moved on to a new project—building a railroad through New York's Adirondack Mountains. He bought up 700,000 acres of wilderness, planning to slice it up and sell it for development as soon as the railroad was done. Luckily for hikers and canoers of the future, he built just sixty miles, then ran out of cash. Today, much of his land is part of Adirondack Park, the largest park in any state except Alaska.

Percy Ebbutt, the ten-year-old pioneer from Britain, left his family's Kansas farm when he was fourteen. "Good-bye, Jack," he wrote to his brother. "Don't wait for me, for I'm not coming home anymore." He spent a couple of years traveling and working, then headed east. When a Philadelphia con man tried to steal his hard-earned cash, Ebbutt used a trick he'd learned in the Wild West. He put his hand into his pocket, "as though I had a revolver," he explained. "Look here," he told the crook, "if you don't hand over my coins in about two shakes, I'll let daylight into you." Ebbutt got his money. Then he boarded a ship and sailed back to London.

After getting fired in Abilene, Kansas, the gunfighter and lawman **James "Wild Bill" Hickok** was desperate for money. He drifted east, took a job in a Wild West show, hated it, and quit. Back in the West he married a former tightrope walker named Agnes Lake. "My eyes are getting real bad," he admitted. "My shooting days are over." Hickok's new plan to support the family: win money gambling. But he'd make lots of enemies over the years, and while he was playing poker in a saloon in Deadwood, Dakota Territory, a man snuck up behind him and shot him in the head. (Poker fans may know that Hickok was holding two aces and two eights—forever after known as the "dead man's hand.")

After leading Texans to victory in their war for independence, **Sam Houston** was elected president of the Republic of Texas in 1836. He later served as a U.S. senator from Texas, and then governor of the state—the only person ever to be governor of two different states (Tennessee and Texas). As tensions between North and South threatened to explode into Civil War, Houston pleaded with both sides to avoid disaster. "I see my beloved South go down in the unequal contest," he predicted, "in a sea of blood and smoking ruin." Texas seceded anyway, and Houston was removed from the governor's job for refusing to swear allegiance to the Confederacy. He died during the Civil War, at the age of seventy.

 When you read short biographies of **Thomas Jefferson,** they usually start by saying that he's the guy who wrote the Declaration of Independence. But right there with the Declaration is his Louisiana Purchase, which changed the whole course of U.S. history. It was popular too, and Jefferson was reelected by a landslide in 1804. He served his second term in the White House, lost pretty much all the popularity he once had, then retired to Virginia and spent seventeen much happier years gardening, renovating his house, founding the University of Virginia, and writing letters (as many as 1,200 per year). He died at home in 1826.

 In 1879 **Chief Joseph** traveled to Washington, D.C., to try to get the government to honor its promise to let the Nez Perce settle on a reservation in their traditional territory. "I only ask of the government to be treated as all other men are treated," Joseph said. Six years later, the Nez Perce were allowed to return to the Northwest—but Joseph was denied the right to live on the reservation in Nez Perce land (the government still considered him dangerous). In 1904, on a reservation in northern Washington, Joseph lay in his tepee, dying. He asked his wife to bring him his old chief's headdress. "I may die at any time," he said, "and I want to die as a chief." She went to get it, but Joseph passed away before she returned. The American doctor on the reservation reported an unusual cause of death: "Chief Joseph died of a broken heart."

Meriwether Lewis had a much shorter, sadder career than his old partner, William Clark. Appointed governor of the Louisiana Territory, the brilliant explorer proved to be a terrible politician. Struggling with depression and alcohol abuse, Lewis fought with everyone and was slow to answer official letters. So many people complained that in 1809 he decided he'd better go to Washington, D.C., to defend his reputation. On the way, he stopped at a tavern in a clearing in the woods in Tennessee. The innkeeper, Priscilla Grinder, later said that Lewis behaved strangely at dinner, and that he "had eaten only a few mouthfuls when he started up, speaking to himself in a violent manner." Later that night Grinder heard a gunshot. Then she heard Lewis cry, "Oh, Lord!" Then another gunshot. Lewis was found lying on his bed, with a hole in his skull so big she could see his brains. He was just thirty-five. Both Thomas Jefferson and William Clark believed Lewis had committed suicide. But Lewis's family was convinced he was murdered, either by political enemies or robbers (he had been carrying $125; it was never found). No one knows what really happened.

When most people think of **Abraham Lincoln** they think of the Civil War, or ending slavery, or that crazy beard—not the West. Lincoln always thought of himself as a westerner, though (Illinois was the West when he was a young man), and he had a major impact on western history. As president, Lincoln pushed hard for construction of the transcontinental railroad. He also signed the Homestead Act, under which the government gave people 270 million acres of western land—that's 10 percent of the entire United States. After he was assassinated in 1865, a train carried his body back west to Illinois, where he was buried.

"After quitting the cowboy life I struck out for Denver," remembered the newly retired cowboy **Nat Love.** "Here I met and married the present Mrs. Love." Then he looked for a job. When city life proved too boring, Love found work as a porter on Pullman railroad cars—one of the few decent jobs open to African American men in those days. He had a bit of trouble on his first day: "I succeeded in getting the shoes of passengers, which had been given to me to polish, badly mixed up," he recalled. "This naturally caused a good-sized rumpus the next morning. And sundry blessings were heaped on the head of yours truly." Love figured out the job, worked fifteen more years, saw the country, and retired in Los Angeles, where he wrote his amazing autobiography, *The Life and Adventures of Nat Love.*

Biddy Mason, the formerly enslaved woman who won her freedom in a California court, settled in Los Angeles, where she began working as a nurse and midwife. In 1866, after ten years of hard work and frugal living, Mason bought her first piece of L.A. real estate (it cost her $250). With a few more years of smart buying and selling, Mason built a fortune, becoming one of the richest women in the West. She built a day care center and a church, and gave so much money to local charities that hungry people, black and white, heard about her generosity and often lined up outside her house to ask for help. Mason died in L.A. at the age of seventy-three.

While running for president in 1844, **James K. Polk** promised that if elected he'd serve only one term. Polk accomplished his major goals of securing American control of Texas, Oregon, and the rest of the West. Then he did something truly amazing—he kept a campaign promise. Refusing calls to run for reelection, Polk retired to his home in Tennessee in 1849. Exhausted and sick (turns out he had cholera), Polk died later that year—giving him the sad distinction of enjoying the shortest retirement (104 days) of any president in American history.

 "**Red Cloud,** the famous old Sioux Indian chief, is dead." That was the first sentence of a small article in the *New York Times* on December 11, 1909. Though he had led the most successful war ever fought by Native Americans against the United States, Red Cloud was unable to win lasting freedom for his people or himself. He lived the last thirty-five years of his life on reservations. Still a respected leader, Red Cloud spent much of that time arguing passionately against the U.S. government's plans to break reservations into smaller and smaller pieces. "They made us many promises, more than I can remember," Red Cloud said of the government. "But they never kept but one; they promised to take our land, and they took it."

 The thirteen-year-old Donner Party survivor **Virginia Reed** settled with her family in California. When she was sixteen she fell in love with a young man named John Murphy. They wanted to marry, but Virginia's father vowed, according to a newspaper report, "that he would shoot Murphy if he dared attempt a marriage." "Sir, you may shoot me," Murphy responded. "But I shall marry your daughter." One night soon after, Virginia told her mother she was going across the street to a friend's house. There she met Murphy and they were secretly (and very quickly) married. And it worked out—they had nine children. Virginia Reed died in 1921, at the age of eighty-seven.

 History loses touch with **Sacagawea** soon after the Lewis and Clark Expedition.

Some sources report that she traveled west and rejoined the Shoshone, living happily with them until her death in 1884. But scholars who have spent time looking for clues say it's much more likely that she died in 1812 at a fort in what is now South Dakota. In December of that year, a clerk at the fort wrote in his diary that the "wife of Charbonneau" had just died of fever. "She was a good and the best woman in the fort, age about 25," wrote the clerk. Sacagawea would have been about twenty-five by 1812. One other piece of evidence: in 1820 William Clark wrote a report with updates on the members of his expedition. For Sacagawea, he wrote "dead."

We know more about Sacagawea's son, Jean Baptiste, who crossed the West with Lewis and Clark as an infant. William Clark became his legal guardian and enrolled him in school in St. Louis. Jean Baptiste learned four languages and traveled the world before returning to the West and working as a fur trapper, mountain guide, and gold miner. He was on his way to search for gold in Montana when he died in 1866, age sixty-one.

 After watching her parents die on the Oregon Trail, then witnessing the death of her adoptive parents in the Whitman massacre, life calmed down a bit for thirteen-year-old **Catherine Sager.** She spent her teen years with a new family in Oregon, then married a minister named Clark Pringle, settled in Spokane, Washington, and had eight children. In her spare time she wrote an account of her adventures as a girl, planning to use the profits from book sales to build an orphanage. Incredibly, no one wanted to publish her story (what, not dramatic enough?). Catherine died in 1910, at the age of seventy-five, but her children saved her writing, and today you can (and should) read her book—it's called *Across the Plains in 1844.*

After losing Texas and the rest of the West to the Americans, **Antonio López de Santa Anna** spent a few years in exile, then returned to Mexico City and regained the presidency. Now calling himself dictator for life (also "Most Serene Highness") he pocketed millions in government money before being booted out yet again in 1855. He then drifted from Cuba to Colombia to New York City. Searching for a get-rich-quick scheme (to fund another attempt to take power in Mexico), he imported a shipment of *chicle*—a natural gum from Central American trees. His plan: find a way to turn chicle into rubber for carriage tires. This failed, but an American friend, Thomas Adams, mixed Santa Anna's chicle with sugar and flavor, shaped it into balls, and sold it in drugstores as "chewing gum." A new industry was born, though Santa Anna never saw a penny. He died broke and nearly forgotten in 1876.

After retiring from the army in 1884, **William Tecumseh Sherman** was so popular that Republican leaders started talking about nominating him for president. The general was not interested. "If nominated I will not run," he grunted. "If elected I will not serve." After years of harsh and merciless war, Sherman retired to New York City, took up paint-ing, and spent his time going to dinner parties and the theater. The major danger facing him now was that crowds of excited admirers followed him everywhere. In 1886 he shook so many hands that he broke a bone in his right hand. The next year he lost two fingernails. Sherman survived the mobs (and admitted privately that he loved the fame). He died in New York in 1891, at age seventy-one.

 At the age of seventy, **Benjamin Singleton** could have slowed down a bit. But the man who helped spark the Exoduster movement kept urging black families to move west, encouraging them to combine their resources to start black-owned factories and schools. He spent so much money travel-ing and printing posters that he was always broke. On his seventy-third birthday, friends threw him a huge party in a park in Topeka, Kansas, asking everyone to donate a little something to the guest of honor. "Any-thing in the way of eatables will be kindly received," Singleton added. He lived another nine years, always proud of his work, and especially proud of his nickname: "Father of the Exodus."

 Soon after the discovery of gold near **John Sutter**'s mill in California in 1848, all Sutter's workers abandoned their jobs and raced off for the diggings. Then, as gold fever at-tracted miners from around the world, thousands swarmed onto Sutter's land, trampling his crops and eating his cows. By 1852 Sut-ter's vast empire was gone. "Without having discovered the gold, I would have become the richest man on the Pacific shore," moaned Sutter. He moved east and spent the last fifteen years of his life pleading with Con-gress to compensate him for his stolen land. It never happened—Sutter died in a cheap Washington, D.C., hotel in 1880.

His victories in the U.S.-Mexican War made General **Zachary Taylor** a national hero. Affectionately nicknamed "Old Rough and Ready" (based on his sloppy appearance, plus the fact he always seemed ready to fight), Taylor was elected president in 1848. After spending the long, hot day of July 4, 1850, attending Independence Day celebrations, a terribly thirsty Taylor downed enormous amounts of cold milk and cherries. He was up all night with intense stomach pains—and died just five days later. Doctors suspected heatstroke or severe diarrhea. But stories spread that his cherries had been poisoned with arsenic. The rumors never died, and in 1991 Taylor's remains were dug up and scientists tested his hair and fingernails. They did find some traces of arsenic (most people have a tiny bit in their bodies), but not nearly enough to have killed him.

 As a Mexican leader in California, **Mariano Guadalupe Vallejo** had always welcomed American immigrants. When the Americans took over, Vallejo was tossed in prison for two months (though he was never charged with having done anything illegal). When he got out, Vallejo helped write California's new state constitution and was elected to the state senate. But he was powerless to stop the flood of settlers onto his land. According to the treaty made with Mexico at the end of the U.S.-Mexican War, Mexicans who owned land in California would still own their land under U.S. law. Vallejo spent years in court trying to protect his rights, but he never got his land back. Once the owner of 250,000 acres, Vallejo moved into a small house on his last 300 acres. "What a difference between then and now," he said. "Then, youth, strength, riches; now age, weakness, and poverty."

The young Nez Perce warrior **Yellow Wolf** was not captured along with Chief Joseph. He slipped out of camp, raced toward Canada, and caught up with other escaping Nez Perce—including his mother and Joseph's twelve-year-old daughter. Yellow Wolf lived in Canada until the following spring, when he got homesick and returned to the Wallowa Valley. "The places through which I was riding came to my heart," he said. "My friends, my brothers, my sisters! All were gone! No tepees anywhere along the river. I was all alone." Considered a fugitive from the law, Yellow Wolf was chased by soldiers and decided to turn himself in. He was eventually sent to the Colville Reservation in Washington, along with Chief Joseph. He lived there nearly fifty years, dying in 1935, at the age of seventy-nine.

 The government rewarded all the members of the Lewis and Clark Expedition with land and money—all except **York**. York was still enslaved, which meant he was legally entitled to nothing. Given his valuable services to Clark and to the country, York had the nerve to ask for his freedom. Clark refused. York asked at least to be sent, as a slave, to Louisville, Kentucky, where his wife was enslaved. Clark refused (agreeing only to allow York to visit his wife for three weeks). What happened next? Some believe York died in slavery. Others say York worked for Clark another ten years, was finally freed, and settled in Kentucky. Still others believe he escaped and headed west—in 1834 one witness claimed to have seen him living with the Crow Indians in Wyoming. The real fate of York is a mystery still to be solved. That seems like a good way to end the book, doesn't it?

Source Notes

When I started researching this book on the West, the problem wasn't finding sources—it was finding *too many* sources. A history nerd like myself (actually I prefer to think of myself as a "story detective") can get so excited about exploring all the amazing stories that he never actually writes a book. Or gets paid. What I'm trying to say is that I went through a lot of books. Below is a list of the books and others sources in which I found all the great stuff you read in this book (you did read it, right?). I hope it's helpful.

Books about the West

As always, I started by reading books that give an overview of all the action and major players. These books cover America's westward expansion, Indians, mountain men, miners, cowboys, pioneers, railroads, and lots more. They also introduced me to tons of great characters—people I made sure to find out more about in other books.

Barnard, Edward S. *Reader's Digest: Story of the Great American West*. Pleasantville, N.Y.: Reader's Digest Association, 1977.

Lavender, David. *The Great West*. New York: American Heritage, 1985.

Stegner, Page. *Winning the Wild West: The Epic Saga of the American Frontier, 1800–1899*. New York: Free Press, 2002.

Utley, Robert M., ed. *The Story of the West: A History of the American West and Its People*. New York: DK Pub., 2003.

Ward, Geoffrey C. *The West: An Illustrated History*. Boston: Little, Brown, 1996.

Wexler, Alan. *Atlas of Westward Expansion*. New York: Facts on File, 1995.

Books and articles about territorial expansion and trails west

The sources here cover a lot of ground (literally). They're all about the rapid expansion of United States, along with stories about early American traders, travelers, and settlers. Speaking of expansion of the United States, how come no one's ever made a movie (a comedy, I mean) about Livingston and Monroe in Paris, trying to figure out if they should buy half a continent from France? Hey, I'd see it.

Ambrose, Stephen. *Undaunted Courage: Meriwether Lewis, Thomas Jefferson, and the Opening of the American West.* New York: Simon & Schuster, 1996.

Brands, H. W. *Lone Star Nation: How a Ragged Army of Volunteers Won the Battle for Texas Independence—and Changed America.* New York: Doubleday, 2004.

Cerami, Charles. *Jefferson's Great Gamble: The Remarkable Story of Jefferson, Napoleon, and the Men Behind the Louisiana Purchase.* Naperville, Ill.: Sourcebooks, 2003.

Christensen, Carol and Thomas. *The U.S.-Mexican War: Companion to the Public Television Series, The U.S.-Mexican War, 1846–1848.* San Francisco: Bay Books, 1998.

Corbett, Christopher. *Orphans Preferred: The Twisted Truth and Lasting Legend of the Pony Express.* New York: Broadway Books, 2003.

Dary, David. *The Oregon Trail: An American Saga.* New York: Knopf, 2004.

———. *The Santa Fe Trail: Its History, Legends, and Lore.* New York: Knopf, 2000.

Eisenhower, John S. D. *So Far from God: The U.S. War with Mexico, 1846–1848.* New York: Random House, 1989.

Golay, Michael. *The Tide of Empire: America's March to the Pacific.* Hoboken, N.J.: Wiley, 2003.

Hansen, Todd, ed. *The Alamo Reader: A Study in History.* Mechanicsburg, Penn.: Stackpole Books, 2003.

Hyslop, Stephen. *Bound for Santa Fe: The Road to New Mexico and the American Conquest, 1806–1848.* Norman: University of Oklahoma Press, 2002.

Kukla, Jon. *A Wilderness So Immense: The Louisiana Purchase and the Destiny of America.* New York: Knopf, 2003.

Leckie, Robert. *From Sea to Shining Sea: From the War of 1812 to the Mexican War, the Saga of America's Expansion.* New York: HarperCollins, 1993.

Lyon, E. Wilson. *The Man Who Sold Louisiana: The Career of Francois Barbé-Marbois.* Norman: University of Oklahoma Press, 1942.

Matovina, Timothy, ed. *The Alamo Remembered: Tejano Accounts and Perspectives.* Austin: University of Texas Press, 1995.

McLynn, Frank. *Wagons West: The Epic Story of America's Overland Trails.* London: Jonathan Cape, 2002.

Morris, Larry E. *The Fate of the Corps: What Became of the Lewis and Clark Explorers After the Expedition.* New Haven: Yale University Press, 2004.

O'Sullivan, John. "Annexation." *United States Magazine and Democratic Review* 17, no. 1 (July–August 1845): PP NOs.

Ronda, James P. *Lewis & Clark Among the Indians.* Lincoln: University of Nebraska Press, 1984.

Schlissel, Lillian. *Women's Diaries of the Westward Journey.* New York: Schocken Books, 1982.

Stewart, George R. *Ordeal by Hunger: The Story of the Donner Party.* New York: H. Holt and Co., 1936.

Tucker, Robert W., and William C. Henderson. *Empire of Liberty: The Statecraft of Thomas Jefferson.* New York: Oxford University Press, 1992.

Utley, Robert M. *A Life Wild and Perilous: Mountain Men and the Paths to the Pacific.* New York: Henry Holt, 1997.

Webb, Walter Prescott. *The Handbook of Texas.* Austin: Texas State Historical Society, 1952.

Books and sources on the gold rush and miners

If you were an American in 1849, do you think you'd have joined the gold rush? I'm betting most miners would probably have stayed home if they'd known how hard it was going to be to strike it rich. Too bad for them that they couldn't read the books below—all about how hard it was to strike it rich. These sources also show us how different the gold rush experience was for men and women, and for people from different parts of the world.

Andrist, Ralph K. *American Heritage: The California Gold Rush*. New York: American Heritage Publishing, 1961.

Egenhoff, Elisabeth L. *The Elephant as They Saw It: A Collection of Contemporary Pictures and Statements on Gold Mining in California*. California Division of Mines, 1949.

Holliday, J. S. *Rush for Riches: Gold Fever and the Making of California*. Berkeley: University of California Press, 1999.

————. *The World Rushed In: The California Gold Rush Experience*. New York: Simon & Schuster, 1981.

Johnson, Susan Lee. *Roaring Camp: The Social World of the California Gold Rush*. New York: W. W. Norton & Co., 2000.

Ketchum, Liza. *The Gold Rush*. Boston: Little, Brown, 1996.

Lapp, Rudolph M. *Blacks in Gold Rush California*. New Haven: Yale University Press, 1977.

Lavender, David. *The Rockies*. New York: Harper & Row, 1975.

Lavoie, Steven. "Wimmer's Nugget." Online article at Oakland Museum of California website, www.museumca.org/goldrush/ar08.html.

Levy, Jo Ann. *They Saw the Elephant: Women in the California Gold Rush*. Norman: University of Oklahoma Press, 1992.

Perl, Lila. *To the Golden Mountain*. Tarrytown, N.Y.: Benchmark Books, 2003.

Ridge, John Rollin. *The Life and Adventures of Joaquin Murieta, the Celebrated California Bandit*. Norman: University of Oklahoma Press, 1955.

Walker, Dale L. *Eldorado: The California Gold Rush*. New York: Tom Doherty Associates, 2003.

Wallace, Robert. *The Old West: The Miners*. New York: Time Life Books, 1976.

Yung, Judy, Gordon H. Chang, and Him Mark Lai, eds. *Chinese American Voices: From the Gold Rush to the Present*. Berkeley: University of California Press, 2006.

Books about railroad building

Way back when I started this project, my idea was to make the whole book about the building of the transcontinental railroad. So, maybe it wasn't a great idea. But you have to admit, the railroad race was exciting stuff, and actually getting the thing built was one of the great engineering feats of all time. These books tell all about the people who pulled it off.

Ambrose, Stephen E. *Nothing Like It in the World: The Men Who Built the Transcontinental Railroad.* New York: Simon & Schuster, 2000.

Bain, David Howard. *Empire Express: Building the First Transcontinental Railroad.* New York: Viking, 1999.

Blumberg, Rhoda. *Full Steam Ahead: The Race to Build a Transcontinental Railroad.* Washington, D.C.: National Geographic Society, 1996.

Brown, Dee. *Hear That Lonesome Whistle Blow: Railroads in the West.* New York: Holt, Rinehart and Winston, 1977.

Coolidge, Susan. "A few hints on the California Journey." *Scribner's,* vol. 6, May 1873.

Earl, Phillip. *This Was Nevada.* Reno: Nevada Historical Society, 1986.

Grenville, Dodge. *How We Built the Union Pacific Railway.* Washington, D.C.: U.S. Government Printing Office, 1910.

Jenson, Oliver Ormerod. *The American Heritage History of Railroads in America.* New York: Random House, 1994.

Klein, Maury. *Union Pacific: Volume I, 1862–1893.* Minneapolis: University of Minnesota Press, 2006.

Mayer, Lynne Rhodes, and Ken Vose. *Makin' Tracks: The Saga of the Transcontinental Railroad.* New York: Barnes & Noble Books, 1975.

Seymour, Silas. *Incidents of a Trip Through the Great Platte Valley.* New York: D. Van Norstrant, 1867.

Williams, John Hoyt. *A Great and Shining Road: The Epic Story of the Transcontinental Railroad.* New York: Times Books, 1988.

Books and articles about pioneers and cowboys

What do you think was harder, being a cowboy or a homesteader? Both seem pretty tiring. Maybe women pioneers had it the toughest. Anyway, the books below give thousands of incredible details about just how challenging life was for cowboys and pioneers—way more good stuff than I could cram into one book.

Conrad, Pam. *Prairie Visions: The Life and Times of Solomon Butcher.* New York: HarperCollins, 1991.

Dick, Everett. *The Sod-House Frontier: 1854–1890*. Lincoln, Neb.: Johnsen Publishing Co., 1954.

Forbis, William H. *The Old West: The Cowboys*. New York: Time Life Books, 1973.

Horn, Hurston. *The Old West: The Pioneers*. New York: Time-Life Books, 1974.

Katz, William Loren. *The Black West*. New York: Simon & Schuster, 1987.

McNeal, Thomas Allen. *When Kansas Was Young*. New York: Macmillan Co., 1922.

Miller, Nyle H. "An English Runnymede in Kansas." *Kansas Historical Quarterly* 41 (1975): PP. Nos.

Nebraska Society of the Daughters of the American Revolution. *Nebraska Pioneer Reminiscences*. Cedar Rapids, Iowa: Torch Press, 1916.

Painter, Nell Irving. *Exodusters: Black Migration to Kansas After Reconstruction*. New York: Knopf, 1977.

Stratton, Joanna L. *Pioneer Women: Voices from the Kansas Frontier*. New York: Simon & Schuster, 1981.

Books about Native Americans and the Indian wars

These books tell some of the most interesting, exciting—and depressing—stories in American history. What's great about these sources is that they include the Indian point of view of key events, as well as direct quotes, memories, and stories from Native American participants.

Andrist, Ralph K. *The Long Death: The Last Days of the Plains Indians*. N.Y.: Collier Books, 1964.

Brown, Dee. *Bury My Heart at Wounded Knee: An Indian History of the American West*. New York: Holt, Rinehart & Winston, 1970.

Coutant, C. G. *The History of Wyoming*, vol. 1. Laramie, Wyo.: Chaplin, Spafford & Mathison, 1899.

Fort Laramie Treaty, 1868. The Avalon Project at Yale Law School.

Goodrich, Thomas. *Scalp Dance: Indian Warfare on the High Plains, 1865–1879*. Mechanicsburg, Pa.: Stackpole Books, 2002.

Grinnell, George Bird. *The Fighting Cheyennes*. Norman: University of Oklahoma Press, 1956.

Hoig, Stan. *The Sand Creek Massacre*. Norman: University of Oklahoma Press, 1961.

Hyde, George E. *Life of George Bent: Written from His Letters*. Norman: University of Oklahoma Press, 1968.

Nerburn, Kent. *Chief Joseph & the Flight of the Nez Perce*. San Francisco: Harper-SanFrancisco, 2005.

Olson, James C. *Red Cloud and the Sioux Problem*. Lincoln: University of Nebraska Press, 1965.

"Red Cloud, Sioux Chief, Dead." *New York Times,* December 11, 1909.

Stefoff, Rebecca. *American Voices from the Wild West*. Tarrytown, N.Y.: Marshall Cavendish, 2006.

Biographies of key figures in the history of the West

This book features a huge and diverse cast of characters. I tried pretty hard to search out quotes and stories to make key characters come alive. Here are some of the sources that I found most helpful.

Ambrose, Stephen. *Crazy Horse and Custer: The Parallel Lives of Two American Warriors*. New York: Doubleday, 1975.

Anderson, Irving. W. *A Charbonneau Family Portrait*. NPS booklet.

Bankes, James. "Wild Bill Hickok." *Wild West Magazine*, August 1996.

De Bruhl, Marshall. *Sword of San Jacinto: A Life of Sam Houston*. New York: Random House, 1993.

Fellman, Michael. *Citizen Sherman: A Life of William Tecumseh Sherman*. Lawrence: University of Kansas Press, 1995.

Fleming, Walter L. "Pap Singleton, The Moses of the Colored Exodus." *American Journal of Sociology* 15 (July 1909): PP Nos.

Foote, Shelby. *The Civil War: A Narrative*, vol. 3. New York: Random House, 1974.

Graham, W. A. *The Custer Myth: A Source Book of Custeriana*. Mechanicsburg, Pa.: Stackpole Books, 1995.

Leckie, Shirley A. *Elizabeth Bacon Custer and the Making of a Myth*. Norman: University of Oklahoma Press, 1993.

Rosa, Joseph G. *Wild Bill Hickok: The Man & His Myth*. Lawrence: University Press of Kansas, 1996.

Sandburg, Carl. *Abraham Lincoln: The Prairie Years and the War Years,* 1-vol. ed. New York: Harcourt, Brace & World, 1954.

Seigenthaler, John. *James K. Polk, 1845–1849*. The American Presidents. New York: Times Books, 2003.

Thomasma, Kenneth. *The Truth About Sacagawea*. Jackson, Wyo.: Grandview Publishing Co., 1997.

Utley, Robert. *The Lance and the Shield: The Life and Times of Sitting Bull*. New York: Ballantine Books, 1993.

"Virginia Reed Elopes." *Illinois Journal*, April 16, 1850.

Williams, Jean Kinney. *Bridget "Biddy" Mason*. Minneapolis: Compass Point Books, 2006.

Memoirs and other firsthand accounts by participants

These sources were by far the most important to me in writing this book—which explains why the list is so long. And you don't always have to go to libraries to search for this stuff. These days you can find many of these texts online at the Library of Congress site (www.loc. gov) or at the websites of universities. Though sometimes I read a book online and loved it so much I just had to order a real copy, like with Preuss's *Exploring with Frémont* and James Beckwourth's *Adventures*. Hey, I said I was a history nerd. I mean, story detective.

Abbott, E. C. *We Pointed Them North: Recollections of a Cowpuncher*. New York: Farrar & Rinehart, 1939.

Beckwourth, James P. *The Life and Adventures of James P. Beckwourth*. New York: Harper & Brothers, 1856.

Black Elk. *Black Elk Speaks: The Life Story of a Holy Man of the Oglala Sioux, as told to John G. Neihardt*. New York: MJF Books, 1932.

Brown, James S. *California Gold: An Authentic History of the First Find with the Names of Those Interested in the Discovery*. Salt Lake City: Pacific Press Publishing Co., 1894.

Carson, J. H. *Early Recollections of the Mines*. Pamphlet published in *San Joaquin Republican*, 1852.

Chivington, John M. "Reports of Col. John M. Chivington," in *The War of the Rebellion: A Compilation of the Official Records of the Union and Confeder-*

ate Armies, vol. 41. Washington, D.C.: United States War Department, 1893.

———. "Testimony of Colonel J. M. Chivington." Joint Committee on the Conduct of the War, Massacre of Cheyenne Indians, 38th Cong., 2nd sess. (Washington, 1865), pp. 4–12, 56–59, 101–8.

Christman, Enos. *One Man's Gold: The Letters and Journal of a Forty-niner.* New York: McGraw-Hill, 1930.

Clark, William, and Meriwether Lewis. *The Journals of the Lewis and Clark Expedition.* Edited by Gary E. Moulton. Lincoln: University of Nebraska Press, 1983.

Clyman, James. "Narrative by James Clyman," original manuscript owned by the State Historical Society of Wisconsin, CITY.

Custer, Elizabeth B. *Boots and Saddles, or Life in Dakota with General Custer.* New York: Harper & Brothers, 1885.

———. *Following the Guidon.* New York: Harper & Brothers, 1890.
Donner, Elizabeth. *The Expedition of the Donner Party and Its Tragic Fate.* Los Angeles: Grafton Publishing Co., 1920.

Ebutt, Percy G. *Emigrant Life in Kansas.* London: S. Sonnenschein and Co., 1886.

Howard, Oliver O. *My Life and Experiences Among Our Hostile Indians.* Hartford, Conn.: A. D. Worthington & Co., 1907.

Howard, William Willard. "The Rush to Oklahoma." *Harper's Weekly,* May 18, 1889.

Jackson, Donald, ed. *Letters of the Lewis and Clark Expedition, with Related Documents,* vol. 1. Urbana: University of Illinois Press, 1978.

Jefferson, Thomas. *The Writings of Thomas Jefferson,* vol. 6. Washington, D.C.: Taylor and Maury, 1854.

Chief Joseph. "An Indian's View of Indian Affairs." North American Review, April 1879.

Kip, Leonard. *California Sketches, with Recollections of the Gold Mines.* Albany, N.Y.: E.H. Pease & Co., 1850.

Knapp, Louise Amelia. *The Shirley Letters from California Mines in 1851–52.* San Francisco: Printed by T. C. Russell, 1922.

Knower, Daniel. *The Adventures of a Forty-niner: An Historic Description of California, with Events and Ideas of San Francisco and Its people in Those Early Days.* Published by the author, 1894.

Leeper, David Rohrer. *The Argonauts of Forty-nine: Some Recollections of the Plains and the Diggings.* South Bend, Ind.: J. B. Stoll & Co., 1894.

Lincoln, Abraham. *Speeches and Writings, 1832–1858.* New York: Library of America, 1989.

Love, Nat. *The Life and Adventures of Nat Love*. Published by the author, Los Angeles, 1907.

Luther Standing Bear. *My People the Sioux*. Lincoln: University of Nebraska Press, 1928.

Marryat, Frank. *Mountains and Molehills, or Recollections of a Burnt Journal*. London: Longman, Brown, Green, and Longmans, 1855.

Mayer, Frank H. *The Buffalo Harvest*. Denver: Sage Books, 1958.

Meriwether, David. *My Life in the Mountains and on the Plains*. Norman: University of Oklahoma Press, 1965.

Megquier, Mary Jane. *Apron Full of Gold: The Letters of Mary Jane Megquier from San Francisco, 1849–1856*. San Marino, Calif.: Huntington Library, 1949.

Polk, James K. *The Diary of a President, 1845–1849*. New York: Longmans, Green and Co., 1929.

Preuss, Charles. *Exploring with Frémont: The Private Diaries of Charles Preuss*. Norman: University of Oklahoma Press, 1958.

Pringle, Catherine Sager. Across the Plains in 1844. Pamphlet, 1860.

Reed, Virginia. *Across the Plains in the Donner Party: A Personal Narrative of the Overland Trip to California*. Published by the author, 1891.

Ruede, Howard. *Sod-house Days: Letters from a Kansas Homesteader, 1877–78*. Lawrence: University Press of Kansas, 1937.

Ryan, William Redmond. *Personal Adventures in Upper and Lower California, in 1848–49*. London: W. Shoberl, 1850.

Sanford, Mollie Dorsey. *Mollie: The Journal of Mollie Dorsey Sanford in Nebraska and Colorado Territories*. Lincoln: University of Nebraska Press, 1959.

Seymour, Silas. *Incidents of a Trip Through the Great Platte Valley*. New York: D. Van Nostrand, 1867.

Singleton, Benjamin. Testimony of Benjamin Singleton before the Senate Select Committee Investigating the "Negro Exodus from the Southern States." Washington, D.C., April 17, 1880.

Siringo, Charles A. *A Texas Cowboy*. Lincoln: University of Nebraska Press, 1950; reprint of 1886 edition.

Stanley, Henry M. *My Early Travels and Adventures*, vol. 1. New York: Charles Scribner's Sons, 1895.

Summerhayes, Martha. *Vanished Arizona: Recollections of My Army Life*. Salem, MA: The Salem Press, 1911.

Sutter, John. *The Diary of Joann August Sutter*. San Francisco: Grabhorn Press, 1932.

———. "The Discovery of Gold in California." *Hutchings' California Magazine*, November 1857.

Svendsen, Gro. *Frontier Mother: The Letters of Gro Svendsen.* Translated and edited by Pauline Farseth and Theodore C. Blegen. Northfield, Minn.: Norwegian-American Historical Association, 1950.

Taylor, Creed. *Tall Men with Long Rifles. Set Down and Written out by James T. DeShields as told to him by Creed Taylor.* San Antonio: Naylor Co., 1971.

Toponce, Alexander. *Reminiscences of Alexander Toponce: Pioneer, 1839–1923.* Published by Mrs. Katie Toponce, Ogden, Utah, 1923.

Twain, Mark. *Roughing It.* New York: Harper & Brothers Publishers, 1871.

Vallejo, Guadalupe. "Ranch and Mission Days in Atla California." *Century Magazine,* December 1890.

Vallejo, Mariano Guadalupe. *Historical and Personal Memoirs Relating to Alta, California.* Translated by Earl R. Hewitt, 5 Vols. Bancroft Library, University of California Berkeley, 1875.

Whitman, Narcissa, and Eliza Spalding. *Where Wagons Could Go.* Edited by Clifford Merrill Drury. Lincoln: University of Nebraska Press, 1997.

Wilson, Elijah Nicholas. *Among the Shoshones.* Salt Lake City: Skelton Publishing Co., 1910.

———. *The White Indian Boy.* Yonkers, NY: World Book Company, 1926.

Wilson, Luzena Stanley. *Luzena Stanley Wilson, '49er: Memories Recalled Years Later for Her Daughter Correnah Wilson Wright.* Mills College, Calif.: Eucalyptus Press, 1937.

Yellow Wolf. *Yellow Wolf: His Own Story.* Caldwell, Idaho.: Caxton Printers, 1940.

Quotation Notes

I used a lot of quotes in my books *King George: What Was His Problem?* and *Two Miserable Presidents*, which were about the American Revolution and the Civil War (and which I highly recommend, by the way—I'm trying to make a living). But for this book I *really* used a lot of quotes. I wanted to try to tell this complicated story from the point of view of the people who were there, and there were so many people, with so many different points of view! The following list shows you where I found all these great quotes. For more information about the sources, look in the Source Notes.

How the West Moved West

"Every eye in the United States" Jefferson, *The Writings*.
"Would you Americans wish to have" Cerami, *Jefferson's Great Gamble*.
"No. Our wishes extend only" Tucker and Henderson, *Empire of Liberty*.
"I should like to know what" Cerami, *Jefferson's Great Gamble*.
"All France's lands west of the Mississippi" Cerami, *Jefferson's Great Gamble*.
"Make it fifty million then" Cerami, *Jefferson's Great Gamble*.
"Doesn't that look like Barbé-Marbois" Cerami, *Jefferson's Great Gamble*.
"The Great Chief of the seventeen great" Jackson, *Letters of Lewis and Clark*
"We feel much at a loss" Lewis and Clark, *Journals*.
"I felt myself warm" Lewis and Clark, *Journals*.
"Most of the warriors appeared" Lewis and Clark, *Journals*.
"a man of no particular merit" Lewis and Clark, *Journals*.
"The Indian woman recognized" Lewis and Clark, *Journals*.
"I now called to him" Lewis and Clark, *Journals*.
"She jumped up and ran" Lewis and Clark, *Journals*.
"Ocian in View! O! the joy" Lewis and Clark, *Journals*.
"You have shot me" Lewis and Clark, *Journals*.
"Being possessed with a strong desire" Beckwourth, *Life and Adventures*.
"If you have a needle" Clyman, *Narrative*
"*be-has-i-pe-hish-a*" Beckwourth, *Life and Adventures*.

"Gentlemen, that Indian wants" Beckwourth, *Life and Adventures*.

"I had learned from the Indians" Meriwether, *My Life*.

"This was the most miserable" Meriwether, *My Life*

"About night my jailor came" Meriwether, *My Life*

"Every man in Texas is called" Leckie, *From Sea to Shining Sea*.

"The great problem I had" Brands, *Lone Star Nation*.

"FELLOW CITIZENS AND COMPATRIOTS" Leckie, *From Sea to Shining Sea*.

"Colonel Travis! The Mexicans" Leckie, *From Sea to Shining Sea*.

Did Someone Say "Manifest Destiny"?

"It was so dark that we couldn't" Matovina, *The Alamo Remembered*.

"We could hear the Mexican" Matovina, *The Alamo Remembered*.

"The struggle lasted more" Hansen, *Alamo Reader*.

"Great God, Sue" Hansen, *Alamo Reader*.

"The boys were continually" Taylor, *Tall Men*.

"Let us fight fast and hard" Taylor, *Tall Men*.

"I was in a deep sleep" Brands, *Lone Star Nation*.

"I saw His Excellency" Brands, *Lone Star Nation*.

"an unheard of journey for females" Whitman and Spalding, *Where Wagons*.

"Our fuel for cooking" Whitman and Spalding, *Where Wagons*.

"I thought of Mother's bread" Whitman and Spalding, *Where Wagons*.

"Yesterday my horse became" Whitman and Spalding, *Where Wagons*.

"The American claim" O'Sullivan, "Annexation."

"Weather good. Food bad" Preuss, *Exploring*.

"Some of the men tried" Preuss, *Exploring*.

"That fellow knows nothing" Preuss, *Exploring*.

"They immediately served" Preuss, *Exploring*.

"The Oregon fever" Utley, *Life Wild*.

"They do say, gentlemen" Schlissel, *Women's Diaries*.

"Dr. Wilson has determined" Schlissel, *Women's Diaries*.

"During the entire trip" Schlissel, *Women's Diaries*.

"The stench is sometimes" McLynn, *Wagons West*.

"The motion of the wagon" Pringle, *Across the Plains*.

"When performing this feat" Pringle, *Across the Plains*.

"So in twenty-six days" Pringle, *Across the Plains*.

"She spoke kindly" Pringle, *Across the Plains*.

"She would point to one" Ward, *The West*.
"Our ignorance of the route" McLynn, *Wagons West*.
"Every one seemed to live" Vallejo, "Ranch and Mission Days."
"We were the pioneers" Vallejo, "Ranch and Mission Days."
"The young Spanish gentlemen" Vallejo, "Ranch and Mission Days."
"I was a child when we started" Reed, *Across the Plains*.
"When we learned of this" Reed, *Across the Plains*.
"The farther we went up" Reed, *Across the Plains*.
"Even the wind seemed" Donner, *The Expedition*.
"We saw a woman emerge" Stewart, *Ordeal*.
"Are you men from California" Stewart, *Ordeal*.
"We are all very well pleased" Reed, *Across the Plains*.
"If you insist on remaining" Eisenhower, *So Far from God*.

War, Land, Gold, Trouble

"Hostilities have commenced" Eisenhower, *So Far from God*.
"Mexico has passed the boundary" Leckie, *From Sea to Shining Sea*.
"That soil was not ours" Lincoln, *Writings*.
"The principle of waging war" Sandburg, *Abraham Lincoln*.
"Mexico should fight to the end" Christensen, *U.S.-Mexican War*.
"Tell Santa Anna to go" Christensen, *U.S.-Mexican War*.
"I beg leave to say" Christensen, *U.S.-Mexican War*.
"I looked out of my bedroom" Vallejo, *Historical and Personal Memoirs*.
"My wife advised me to try" Vallejo, *Historical and Personal Memoirs*.
"They were about as rough" Christensen, *U.S.-Mexican War*.
"To what happy circumstances" Vallejo, *Historical and Personal Memoirs*.
"The bear was so badly painted" Vallejo, *Historical and Personal Memoirs*.
"A paradise of the lizard" Ward, *The West*.
"I want hard times" Ward, *The West*.
"The poor Indians are amazed" Ward, *The West*.
"The disease was raging" Pringle, Across the Plains.
"Suddenly there was a sharp" Pringle, Across the Plains.
"Did they kill the doctor" Pringle, Across the Plains.
"Then a bullet came" Pringle, Across the Plains.
"I sat upon the side" Pringle, Across the Plains.
"My eye was caught" Walker, *Eldorado*.
"I have found it!" Egenhoff, *The Elephant*.

"It did not seem to be" Walker, *Eldorado*.
"just out of the mouth" Lavoie, "Wimmer's Nugget."
"I will throw it into my" Lavoie, "Wimmer's Nugget."
"He was soaked to the skin" Andrist, *California Gold Rush*.
"like a crazy man" Walker, *Eldorado*.
"Are you alone" Walker, *Eldorado*.
"I declared this to be gold" Sutter, "Discovery of Gold."
"I have made a discovery" Holliday, *World Rushed In*.
"That there is gold" Brown, *California Gold*.
"Gold! Gold! Gold" Walker, *Eldorado*.
"The whole population are going" Ketchum, *Gold Rush*.
"One day I saw a form, bent" Carson, *Early Recollections*.
"My legs performed some entirely" Carson, *Early Recollections*.
"Your streams have minnows" Holliday, *World Rushed In*.
"The gold excitement spread" Wilson, *Memories Recalled*.
"One of our company" Holliday, *World Rushed In*.
"Another insect which is rather" Levy, *They Saw the Elephant*.
"What's the matter" Kip, *California Sketches*.

Welcome to the Wild West

"Do you think I'll lug" Lapp, *Blacks in Gold Rush*.
"This is the best place" Lapp, *Blacks in Gold Rush*.
"What a puzzling place" Kip, *California Sketches*.
"Well, not much" Levy, *They Saw the Elephant*.
"This street is impassable" Walker, *Eldorado*.
"Money here goes like dirt" Christman, *One Man's Gold*.
"Good morning, Firmore" Ryan, *Personal Adventures*.
"But, luck or no luck" Ryan, *Personal Adventures*.
"There is gold here in abundance" Walker, *Eldorado*.
"The chances of making a fortune" Walker, *Eldorado*.
"I am willing to stand" Holliday, *World Rushed In*.
"strewn with old boots" Ketchum, *Gold Rush*.
"My first day's work" Holliday, *World Rushed In*.
"O! William, I cannot wait" Holliday, *World Rushed In*.
"George, I tell you mining" Holliday, *World Rushed In*.
"Boys, what's that" Walker, *Eldorado*.
"I'll give you five dollars" Wilson, *Memories Recalled*.

"Madame, I want a good" Wilson, *Memories Recalled*.
"I, as before, set up my stove" Wilson, *Memories Recalled*.
"He came back in a few" Knower, *Adventures*.
"It is far more pleasing to me" Holliday, *Rush for Riches*.
"It is a painful necessity" Ketchum, *Gold Rush*.
"I was sorry to stab" Perl, *Golden Mountain*.
"Oh, don't ever marry" Yung, Chang, and Lai, *Chinese American*.
"You are the chap" Ridge, *Life and Adventures*.
"I have no pile yet" Holliday, *World Rushed In*.
"I feel bad sometimes" Holliday, *Rush for Riches*.
"Got nearer to a female" Holliday, *World Rushed In*.
"I have made up my mind" Holliday, *World Rushed In*.
"I have been many miles" Holliday, *World Rushed In*.
"I always feared this trip" Williams, *"Biddy" Mason*.
"I went to bed and dreamed" Wallace, *The Miners*.
"a mad, furious race for wealth" Wallace, *The Miners*.
"First we would all be" Twain, *Roughing It*.
"Cal, what kind of house" Twain, *Roughing It*.
"Don't fail to do the work" Twain, *Roughing It*.
"I was absolutely and unquestionably" Twain, *Roughing It*.
"I had once been a grocery" Twain, *Roughing It*.

Out of the Way of the Big Engine

"I was just eighteen" Corbett, *Orphans Preferred*.
"They refused to move" Corbett, *Orphans Preferred*.
"When we started out" Corbett, *Orphans Preferred*.
"He said I had no right" Wilson, *White Indian*.
"One of the Indians shot" Wilson, *White Indian*.
"They got a few men" Wilson, *White Indian*.
"It will be built" Bain, *Empire Express*.
"Theodore, those people" Bain, *Empire Express*.
"Anna, if you want to see" Ambrose, *Nothing Like It*.
"demanded in the interests" Blumberg, *Full Steam Ahead*.
"This is the grandest enterprise" Blumberg, *Full Steam Ahead*.
"Grab a wad of money" Jenson, *History of Railroads*.
"No man can call" Bain, *Empire Express*.
"This part of the road" Ambrose, *Nothing Like It*.

"There is cheating" Klein, *Union Pacific*.
"I kept him up by dipping" Bain, *Empire Express*.
"Little Indian Boy" Blumberg, *Full Steam Ahead*.
"My son weighs 275" Williams, *Great and Shining*.
"I have gone to sleep" Williams, *Great and Shining*.
"I do not like the idea" Bain, *Empire Express*.
"Everybody saw them" Ward, *The West*.
"I determined to strike a blow" Chivington, *Testimony*
"Kill and scalp all" Andrist, *Long Death*.
"It would be murder" Brown, *Bury My Heart*.
"I was still in bed" Hyde, *Life of George Bent*.
"All was confusion" Hyde, *Life of George Bent*.
"Remember the murdered women" Bain, *Empire Express*.
"I was struck in the hip" Hyde, *Life of George Bent*.
"Everyone was crying" Brown, *Bury My Heart*.
"between five hundred and six hundred Indians" Chivington, *Reports*.
"in the most horrible manner" Brown, *Bury My Heart*.
"As to Colonel Chivington" Stefoff, *American Voices*.
"I stand by Sand Creek" Hoig, *Sand Creek Massacre*.
"This was an uncommon thing" Hyde, *Life of George Bent*.
"The white men have crowded" Brown, *Bury My Heart*.
"If the Great Father kept" Ward, *The West*.
"The Great Father sends" Barnard, *Great American West*.
"Give me eighty men" Andrist, *Long Death*.
"I was sixteen years old" Black Elk, *Black Elk Speaks*.
"When they came to the bottom" Black Elk, *Black Elk Speaks*.
"When we see the soldiers" Brown, *Bury My Heart*.
"startled from their slumbers" Seymour, *Incidents of a Trip*.
"We looked at it" Grinnell, *Fighting Cheyennes*.
"We talked of our troubles" Grinnell, *Fighting Cheyennes*.

Race You to Utah

"About nine o'clock" Stanley, *Early Travels*.
"We fired two or three shots" Stanley, *Early Travels*.
"He then took out his knife" Stanley, *Early Travels*.
"I can't describe it to you" Stanley, *Early Travels*.
"The Indian then mounted" Stanley, *Early Travels*.

"In a pail of water" Stanley, *Early Travels*.

"We have had a very anxious day" Ferguson, *Journal*

"We've got to clean" Bain, *Empire Express*.

"No interruption to the work" Brown, *Lonesome Whistle*.

"War is cruelty" Foote, *Civil War*.

"You should not allow" Olson, *Red Cloud*.

"The government of the United States" *Fort Laramie Treaty, 1868*.

"I will not boss Chinese" Williams, *Great and Shining*.

"I was very much prejudiced" Bain, *Empire Express*.

"They did so well" Mayer, *Makin' Tracks*.

"The work was very dangerous" Yung, Chang, and Lai, *Chinese American*.

"Just at that moment" Yung, Chang, and Lai, *Chinese American*.

"We are only averaging" Bain, *Empire Express*.

"Snow slides carried away" Williams, *Great and Shining Road*.

"Some fifteen or twenty" Mayer, *Makin' Tracks*.

"A good many were frozen" Mayer, *Makin' Tracks*.

"Dear Jack, Do get home" Bain, *Empire Express*.

"There are men here" Blumberg, *Full Steam Ahead*.

"We are now sailing" Bain, *Empire Express*.

"Where is it?" Bain, *Empire Express*.

"The line we construct now" Bain, *Empire Express*.

"In truth we became hilarious" Blumberg, *Full Steam Ahead*.

"If the passengers could sleep" Blumberg, *Full Steam Ahead*.

"We must not beat them" Bain, *Empire Express*.

"Everyone had all they wanted" Toponce, *Reminiscences*.

"May God continue" Williams, *Great and Shining Road*.

"Almost ready. Hats off" Bain, *Empire Express*.

"He missed the spike" Toponce, *Reminiscences*.

"The spirit of my brave" Williams, *Great and Shining Road*.

"It was necessary to look" Brown, *Lonesome Whistle*.

"Send me sixty dollars" Earl, *This Was Nevada*.

"Who's there?" Earl, *This Was Nevada*.

"I am very glad" Brown, *Bury My Heart*.

"Telegraph to my people" Brown, *Bury My Heart*.

"I am not dressed" Brown, *Bury My Heart*.

"Surely the white men" Brown, *Bury My Heart*.

"The white children" Olson, *Red Cloud*.

"We want to keep the peace" Brown, *Bury My Heart*.

"I was at that time" Love, *Life and Adventures*.

"A great many saloons" Love, *Life and Adventures*.
"Can you ride a wild horse?" Love, *Life and Adventures*.

Cowboys vs. Farmers

"This proved the worst" Love, *Life and Adventures*.
"I was the poorest" Abbott, *We Pointed Them*.
"The idea was it would" Abbott, *We Pointed Them*.
"The cowboys were mostly" Abbott, *We Pointed Them*.
"We had no tents" Barnard, *Great American West*.
"Should anyone" Barnard, *Great American West*.
"Imagine, my dear reader" Love, *Life and Adventures*.
"We found him among" Abbott, *We Pointed Them*.
"The singing" Abbott, *We Pointed Them*.
"I'm up in the mornin'" Forbis, *The Cowboys*.
"When you add it all up" Abbott, *We Pointed Them*.
"Of course, boy-like" Ebbutt, *Emigrant Life*.
"Harry Parker made" Ebbutt, *Emigrant Life*.
"None of us knew" Ebbutt, *Emigrant Life*.
"If you have made up" Ebbutt, *Emigrant Life*.
"Well, I guess I'm lost" Stratton, *Pioneer Women*.
"I tell you it is no easy work" Ruede, *Sod-house Days*.
"The sweat runs off" Ruede, *Sod-house Days*.
"Sometimes the bull snakes" Stratton, *Pioneer Women*.
"Where'd you get that egg" Conrad, *Prairie Visions*.
"The land that has been" Ebbutt, *Emigrant Life*.
"There was running water" Stegner, *Winning the Wild West*.
"But I had hardly made" Ruede, *Sod-house Days*.
"What could we burn" Stratton, *Pioneer Women*.
"Of course, these Indians" Stratton, *Pioneer Women*.
"I saw with my own" Stratton, *Pioneer Women*.
"Then, as I clapped" Stratton, *Pioneer Women*.
"I quickly mounted" Stratton, *Pioneer Women*.
"There was scarcely" Forbis, *The Cowboys*.
"And then when the cattle" Abbott, *We Pointed*.
"We looked in the window" Abbott, *We Pointed*.
"We all headed for Dodge" Love, *Life and Adventures*.
"While our money lasted" Love, *Life and Adventures*.

"A cowboy named 'Bum'" Stratton, *Pioneer Women*.
"Well, I thought" Abbott, *We Pointed*.
"We like to get up" Forbis, *The Cowboys*.
"I say, Bill, or Mr. Hickok" Rosa, *Wild Bill*.
"The advantage" Barnard, *Great American West*.
"I stole the whole bunch" Brown, *Lonesome Whistle*.
"It is a strange and terrible" Svendsen, *Frontier Mother*.
"While sitting round" Ebbutt, *Emigrant Life*.
"We used to keep" Ebbutt, *Emigrant Life*.
"There was not a hint" Barnard, *Great American West*.
"It seemed as if we were" Stratton, *Pioneer Women*.
"We first saw a glittering" Ebbutt, *Emigrant Life*.
"The ground was covered" Barnard, *Great American West*.
"It was impossible to walk" Ebbutt, *Emigrant Life*.
"Go get your shawls" Stratton, *Pioneer Women*.
"I would then take" Ebbutt, *Emigrant Life*.
"Little legs, dangling high" Stratton, *Pioneer Women*.
"I have twenty scholars" Sanford, *Mollie*.
"At this place I slept" Sanford, *Mollie*.

The Road to Little Bighorn

"They were walking" Mayer, *Buffalo Harvest*.
"I was young, twenty-two" Mayer, *Buffalo Harvest*.
"I have been on a train" Custer, *Following the Guidon*.
"Everything the Kiowa had" Ward, *The West*.
"Let them kill, skin" Brown, *Bury My Heart*.
"The great buffalo slaughter" Love, *Life and Adventures*.
"The whites may get me" Ward, *The West*.
"Our people knew" Black Elk, *Black Elk Speaks*.
"We have discovered a rich" Custer, *Books and Saddles*.
"We have discovered gold" Custer, *Books and Saddles*.
"Rich Mines of Gold" Donovan, *Custer*.
"You should bow" Ward, *The West*.
"I want you to go" Brown, *Bury My Heart*.
"The Black Hills is my land" Ward, *The West*.
"Our sleeping room" Summerhayes, *Vanished Arizona*. <not in sources?>
"Once at midnight" Summerhayes, *Vanished Arizona*.

Quotation Notes

"I think we will" Ward, *The West*.
"The wives and children" Custer, *Books and Saddles*.
"We have not seen" Custer, *Books and Saddles*.
"They both took advantage" Custer, *Books and Saddles*.
"I feel hopeful" Custer, *Books and Saddles*.
"I have but a few" Custer, *Books and Saddles*.
"The largest Indian camp" Donovan, *Custer*.
"We'll find enough Sioux" Donovan, *Custer*.
"I was thirteen years" Black Elk, *Black Elk Speaks*.
"The chargers are coming!" Black Elk, *Black Elk Speaks*.
"I was so shaky" Black Elk, *Black Elk Speaks*.
"I jumped up" Graham, *The Custer Myth*.
"The bullets were" Graham, *The Custer Myth*.
"They came on us" Barnard, *Great American West*.
"It is a good day to fight" Ambrose, *Crazy Horse*.
"Then came the rush" Goodrich, *Scalp Dance*.
"Courage boys, we've got them" Donovan, *Custer*.
"I think they were" Black Elk, *Black Elk Speaks*.
"The shooting was quick" Ambrose, *Crazy Horse*.
"The blood of the people" Brown, *Bury My Heart*.
"We felt terribly alone" Goodrich, *Scalp Dance*.
"Our little group" Custer, *Books and Saddles*.
"Custer killed" Ward, *The West*.
"The worse it gets" Goodrich, *Scalp Dance*.
"I know it looks hard" Goodrich, *Scalp Dance*.
"The thermometer never" Goodrich, *Scalp Dance*.
"I am tired of being" Utley, *Sitting Bull*.
"Wherever we went" Black Elk, *Black Elk Speaks*.
"I want this peace" Donovan, *Custer*.
"Kill him! Kill him" Ambrose, *Crazy Horse*.
"Let me go, my friends" Ambrose, *Crazy Horse*.
"I cried all night" Black Elk, *Black Elk Speaks*.
"You must stop your ears" Ward, *The West*.
"I pressed my father's hand" Ward, *The West*.

The End of the Wild West

"It is a great mistake" Brown, *Bury My Heart*.
"Chief Toohoolhoolzote" Yellow Wolf, *Own Story*.
"You know very well" Brown, *Bury My Heart*.
"Why are you in such" Joseph, *"Indian's View."*
"If you let the time" Joseph, *"Indian's View."*
"I did not want bloodshed" Joseph, *"Indian's View."*
"Toohoolhoolzote talked for war" Joseph, *"Indian's View."*
"I would have given my own" Joseph, *"Indian's View."*
"It was just like two bulldogs" Yellow Wolf, *Own Story*.
"I never went up" Ward, *The West*.
"From that time" Yellow Wolf, *Own Story*.
"You cannot get by us" Brown, *Bury My Heart*.
"We rode on" Yellow Wolf, *Own Story*.
"Thoughts came" Yellow Wolf, *Own Story*.
"That force of yours" Ward, *The West*.
"We knew General Howard" Yellow Wolf, *Own Story*.
"Soldiers! Soldiers" Yellow Wolf, *Own Story*.
"My little daughter" Joseph, *"Indian's View."*
"Six of my men were killed" Joseph, *"Indian's View."*
"If you will come out" Joseph, *"Indian's View."*
"I am tired of fighting" Brown, *Bury My Heart*.
"The Indians are prisoners" Nerburn, *Chief Joseph*.
"Where were you born" Singleton, Testimony.
"What, go back!" Painter, *Exodusters*.
"There is Nicodemus!" Nugent, *American West*.
"The scenery was not" Nugent, *American West*.
"Mr. Horace Capel" Miller, *"English Runnymede."*
"It was startling" Miller, *"English Runnymede."*
"The immense cattle" Love, *Life and Adventures*.
"I surrender this rifle" Utley, *Lance and Shield*.
"I think you had better" Brown, *Bury My Heart*.
"A warrior I have been" Utley, *Lance and Shield*.
"We were all out playing" Horn, *Pioneers*.
"How it cut" Nebraska DAR, *Reminiscences*.
"A cloud of dust" Howard, *"Rush to Oklahoma"*
"Never before" Howard, *"Rush to Oklahoma"*
"Suddenly great excitement" Standing Bear, *My People*.

"When I first heard" Black Elk, *Black Elk Speaks*.

"Indians are dancing" Ward, *The West*.

"What do you want" Brown, *Bury My Heart*.

"You think you are going" Utley, *Lance and Shield*.

"I saw the soldiers" Brown, *Bury My Heart*.

"If they had left him" Brown, *Bury My Heart*.

"We tried to run" Brown, *Bury My Heart*.

"It was a thing to melt" Barnard, *Great American West*.

"There can hardly be said" Turner, *The Frontier*.

"From now on" Abbott, *We Pointed Them*.

"I took a homestead" Abbott, *We Pointed Them*.

"With the march of progress" Love, *Life and Adventures*.

What Ever Happened to . . .

"I had always worked" Abbott, *We Pointed Them North*.

"The prosperity of Texas" Webb, *Handbook of Texas*.

"My relatives told me" Black Elk, *Black Elk Speaks*.

"It is to be lamented" Morris, *Fate of the Corps*.

"It is nothing to be proud of" Twain, letter to Orion and Mary E. Clemens, October 19, 1865. The Mark Twain Papers and Project, The Bancroft Libary, University of California, Berkeley.

"The reports of my death." Twain, *New York Journal*, June 2, 1897.

"I regard Custer's" Leckie, *Elizabeth Bacon Custer*.

"General Custer's name" Leckie, *Elizabeth Bacon Custer*.

"KING OF FRAUDS" Bain, *Empire Express*.

"Good-bye, Jack" Ebbutt, *Emigrant Life in Kansas*.

"My eyes are getting real bad" Bankes, "Wild Bill Hickok."

"I see my beloved South" De Bruhl, *Sword of San Jacinto*.

"I only ask" Joseph, *"Indian's View."*

"I may die" Nerburn, *Chief Joseph*.

"Chief Joseph died" Nerburn, *Chief Joseph*.

"had eaten only" Morris, *Fate of the Corps*.

"After quitting the cowboy life" Love, *Life and Adventures*.

"Red Cloud" "Red Cloud, Sioux Chief, Dead." *New York Times*, December 11, 1909.

"They made us many promises" Brown, *Bury My Heart*.

"that he would shoot Murphy" "Virginia Reed Elopes."

"wife of Charbonneau" Thomasma, *Truth About Sacajawea.*
"If nominated" Fellman, *Citizen Sherman.*
"Anything in the way of eatables" Fleming, "Pap Singleton."
"Without having discovered" Sutter, *Diary.*
"What a difference" Vallejo, *Historical and Personal Memoirs.*
"The places through" Yellow Wolf, *His Own Story.*

Index

Index

Louisiana Purchase: effect on United States, 7; price paid, 7
Lousy Miner, The (song), 89–90
Love, Nat, 141, 159–161, 173, 203, 215, 224
Low Dog, 182
Lyon, Mary, 165–168

M

Mail. *See also* Pony Express: delivery of, 97
Manifest Destiny: defined, 34
Marcks, Lillie, 167
Marcy, Jennie, 157–159
Marshall, James, 64
Mason, Biddy, 90, 224; quoted, 91
Maxfield, James, 89
Mayer, Frank, 169
Megquier, Jenny, 71
Meriwether, David, 19–21
Mexico: ban on slavery, 23; conflict with, 50; declaration of independence, 21; independence from Spain, 22
Mexico City: captured by Americans, 58
Meyer, Frank, 171
Miles, Nelson, 197
Mining techniques: of gold, 79
Monroe, James: negotiations with France and, 5
Mormon religion, 59
Mormon Trail, 59
Mountain Men: as guides on Oregon Trail, 39
Murrieta, Joaquin, 87

N

Native Americans: cultural misunderstandings and, 157; desire to trade, 40–41; fights with, 17–19; gold rush and, 85
New Orleans: American shipping and, 3
New York Herald: on railroads, 108
Nez Perce, 188–189, 197–199; Christianity and, 31
Nueces River: as southern border, 50

O

O'Sullivan, John, 34
"Old Chisholm Trail, The" (song), 149

Olsson, Olof, 163
Oregon: climate and soil, 38
Oregon conflict, 50
Oregon Trail, 39, 60; Catherine Sager on, 41–43; top causes of death on, 40–41

P

Pacific Railroad Act of 1862, 104, 107
Parker, Ely, 139
Pawnees, 118
Pengra, Charlotte: quoted, 41
Peterson, Mathilda, 157
Plains Indians: fall of, 188
Polk, James K., 34, 50, 225
Pony Express, 97–98; failure of, 101–102; Native American warriors and, 100–102
Population: of California, 92; of United States, 214–215
Prentiss, Narcissa, 31
Preuss, Charles, 36
Promontory Summit, Utah, 132

R

Railroads: as threat to Indian life, 119; building through mountains, 126–129; meeting of, 134–136; robbers on, 136–139
Red Cloud, 139–141, 225; quoted, 114
Red Cloud's War, 115, 124–125
Reed, James, 46
Reed, Virginia, 47, 225–226
Reno, Marcus, 181
Rhoads, Daniel, 49
Rhodes, W. H., 131
Rio Grande: as southern border, 50
Robbers: on railroads, 136–139
Rocky Mountain Fur Company, 16
Rocky Mountains: gold rush in, 92
Rosebud Reservation, 209
Roughing It (Clemens), 95
Ruede, Howard, 153, 155–156
Runnymede, Kansas, 202
Russell, Majors & Waddell's Central Overland California & Pike's Peak Express Company, 97
Ryan, William, 78